IMO

INTERNATIONAL MATHEMATICS OLYMPIAD

3

Shraddha Singh

V&S PUBLISHERS

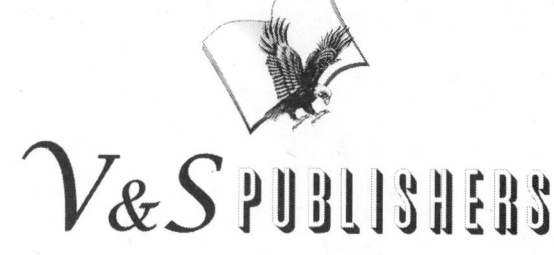

Published by:

V&S PUBLISHERS

F-2/16, Ansari road, Daryaganj, New Delhi-110002
☎ 23240026, 23240027 • *Fax:* 011-23240028
Email: info@vspublishers.com • *Website:* www.vspublishers.com

Regional Office : Hyderabad
5-1-707/1, Brij Bhawan (Beside Central Bank of India Lane)
Bank Street, Koti, Hyderabad - 500 095
☎ 040-24737290
E-mail: vspublishershyd@gmail.com

Branch Office : Mumbai
Jaywant Industrial Estate, 1st Floor–108, Tardeo Road
Opposite Sobo Central Mall, Mumbai – 400 034
☎ 022-23510736
E-mail: vspublishersmum@gmail.com

Follow us on:

All books available at **www.vspublishers.com**

© Copyright: V&S PUBLISHERS
ISBN 978-93-579405-2-8

The Copyright of this book, as well as all matter contained herein (including illustrations) rests with the Publisher. No person shall copy the name of the book, its title design, matter and illustrations in any form and in any language, totally or partially or in any form. Anybody doing so shall face legal action and will be responsible for damages.

Printed at : Param Offseters Okhla New Delhi-110020

Publisher's Note

V&S Publishers, after the grand success of a number of Academic and General books, is pleased to bring out a series of *Mathematics Olympiad books* under *The Gen X series – generating Xcellence in generation X* – which has been designed to focus the problems faced by students. In all books the concepts have been explained clearly through examples, illustrations and diagrams wherever required. The contents have been developed to meet specific needs of students who aspire to get distinctions in the field of mathematics and want to become Olympiad champs at national and international levels.

To go through Maths Olympiad, the students need to do thorough study of topics covered in the *Olympiad syllabus and those covered in the school syllabus as well*. The Olympiads not only tests subjective knowledge but Reasoning skills of students also. So students are required to comprehend the depth of concepts and problems and gain experience through practice. The Olympiad check efficiency of candidates in problem solving. These exams are conducted in different stages at regional, national, and international levels. At each stage of the test, the candidate should be fully prepared to go through the exam. Therefore, this test requires careful attention towards comprehension of concepts, thorough practice, and application of rules.

While other books in market focus selectively on questions or theory; V&S Maths Olympiad books are rather comprehensive. Each book of this series has been divided into four sections namely *Mathematics, Logical Reasoning, Achievers section, Model Papers*. The theory has been explained through solved examples. To enhance the problem solving skills of candidates, *Multiple Choice Questions (MCQs)* with detailed solutions are given at the end of each chapter. Two *Mock Test Papers* have been included to understand the pattern of exam. A CD containing Study Chart for systematic preparation, Tips & Tricks to crack Maths Olympiad, Pattern of exam, and links of Previous Years Papers is accompanied with this book. The books are also useful for various other competitive exams such as NTSE, NSTSE, and SLSTSE as well.

We wish you all success in the examination and a very bright future in the field of mathematics.

All the best

Contents

SECTION 1 : MATHEMATICAL REASONING

1. Number System — 9
2. Addition — 16
3. Subtraction — 22
4. Multiplication — 27
5. Division — 34
6. Fractions — 42
7. Length — 49
8. Weight — 54
9. Capacity — 61
10. Time — 66
11. Money — 72
12. Geometrical Shapes — 79

SECTION 2 : LOGICAL REASONING

1. Pattern — 93
2. Series Completion — 99
3. Odd One Out — 106
4. Coding and Decoding — 112
5. Alphabet Test and Word Formation — 119
6. Problems Based on Figures — 123

SECTION 3 : ACHIEVERS SECTION

High Order Thinking Skills — 131

SECTION 4 : MODEL PAPERS

Model Test Paper – 1 — 135
Model Test Paper – 2 — 139

SECTION 1
MATHEMATICAL REASONING

Unit - 1 : Number System

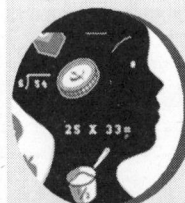

Learning Objectives : In this unit, we will learn about:
- Numerals
- Skip Counting
- Face Value
- Place Value
- Expanded Form
- Number Name
- Ascending Order
- Descending Order
- Number Sense (4 Digit Numbers)
- Even and Odd Numbers
- Regional Numerals

Numerals
The digits 0, 1, 2, 3, 4, 5, 6, 7, 8 and 9 are used to form numbers or numerals. There digits are called ones. The numerals formed by the digits 1, 2, 3, 4 5, 6, 7, 8 and 9 are known as Hindu Arabic numbers.

Skip Counting
Skip counting is counting forward or backward by any number that is not 1. It helps us to count quickly and makes learning of table easier.
Example : Skip counting by 2 is 2, 4, 6, 8, 10 ....

Skip count backward
Count in 3s
30, 27, 24, 21, 18 ....

Skip count forward
Count in 4s
100, 104, 108, 112 ....

Unit - 1 : Number System

Face Value
Face value of a digit in a given number is the digit itself. In the number 452, the face value of 4 is 4, the face value of 5 is 5 and the face value of 2 is 2.

Place Value
The place value of a digit in a given number is the digit multiplied by its place.
Example : Write place value of digit in 264.

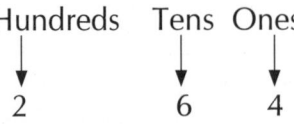

Place value of 2 = 2 × 100 = 200
Place value of 6 = 6 × 10 = 60
Place value of 4 = 4 × 1 = 4

Expanded Form
If a number is written as the sum of the place value of its digits, then it is said to be in expanded form.

Example : Write the expanded form of 356.
Solution : 356 = 3 hundreds + 5 tens + 6 ones
= 3 × 100 + 5 × 10 + 6 × 1
= 300 + 50 + 6

Number Names

Number	Number Names
10	Ten
20	Twenty
50	Fifty
100	Hundred
500	Five Hundred
1000	One Thousand
5000	Five Thousand
10,000	Ten Thousand

Ascending Order
Arranging the given numbers from the smallest to the greatest is called ascending or increasing order.

Descending Order
Arranging the given numbers from the greatest to the smallest is called descending or decreasing order.

Example : Arrange these numbers in descending order and ascending order.
Solution : Here 475   576   311   999   78
         999 > 576 > 475 > 311 > 78
   Decreasing order is 999, 576, 475, 311, 78 and
   Ascending order is 78 , 311, 475, 576, 999

Number Sense (4 Digit Numbers)
We know that there are ten digits: 0, 1, 2, 3, 4, 5, 6, 7, 8, 9. Numbers are written using these digits. These digits are called ones.
The greatest 3 digit number is 999. It can be written as
    999 = 900 + 90 + 9
        = 9 Hundreds + 9 tens + 9 ones
Add 1 to 999 to make a 4 digit number 1 + 999 = 1000
It is the smallest number of four digits. 1000 is the successor of 999.

Even and Odd Numbers
Even numbers
The numbers having 0, 2, 4, 6 ...... at ones place are called even numbers .
Odd numbers
The numbers having 1, 3, 5, 7 .... at ones place are called odd numbers.
    Odd numbers – 11, 13, 15, 19, 23
    Even numbers – 12, 20, 30, 36

Properties of odd and even numbers
1. When we add an even number to an add number the answer is always an odd number.
   Example : 2 + 3 = 5
           Even Odd Odd
2. When we add an odd number to an odd number the answer is always an even number.
   Example : 3 + 5 = 8
           odd odd even
3. When we add two even numbers, the answer is always an even number.
   Example : 2 + 4 = 6
           Even even even

Regional Numerals
Numbers can be written by using different symbols. The numbers represented by particular symbols are known as the digits of the system. Number is an idea whereas the symbols used to represent the numbers are called numerals.

Unit – 1 : Number System

Multiple Choice Questions

1. Which one of the following is the smallest number?
   A. 3116 B. 3316
   C. 3211 D. 3361

2. The place value of 8 in 978353 is
   A. 8000 B. 800
   C. 80 D. 8

3. Which one of the following is correct?
   A. 425 < 238
   B. 9467 > 853
   C. 750 < 915
   D. 525 < 425

4. The sum of two even numbers is
   A. an even number
   B. an add number
   C. both (i) and (ii)
   D. none of these

5. Which place value is used to prove that 5487 is less than 5874?
   A. Ones place
   B. Tens place
   C. Hundreds place
   D. Thousand place

6. Which one of the following is an even number?
   A. 733 B. 550
   C. 241 D. 89

7. Matching of columns

Column I	Column II
(1) 7000 + 400 + 20 + 6	(i) 7067
(2) 7000 + 400 + 0 + 6 + 0	(ii) 766
(3) 700 + 60 + 6	(iii) 7406
(4) 7000 + 0 + 60 + 6 + 7	(iv) 7426

   A. 1 – i, 2 – ii, 3 – iii, 4 – iv
   B. 1 – ii, 2 – iii, 3 – i, 4 – iv
   C. 1 – iv, 2 – iii, 3 – ii, – 4 i
   D. 1 – ii, 2 – iv, 3 – iii, 4 – i

8. A man bought 20 mangoes and distributes them to Sanjay, Ravi, and Vijay. Sanjay gets 5, Ravi gets 6 and Vijay gets _____ mangoes.
   A. 6 B. 7
   C. 8 D. 9

9. The largest 3 digit number is
   A. 999 B. 899
   C. 889 D. 988

10. Find the odd one out.

    14, 2, 12, 5, 10
    A. 2 B. 5
    C. 10 D. 14

Direction (11-12) : A box contains two dozen bananas, 2 apples, 1 pineapple and half dozen mangoes.

11. The total number of fruits in the box are _____.
    A. 21 B. 31
    C. 27 D. 33

12. If three more bananas are added to these fruits, then the total number of fruits in the box will be _____.
    A. 1 Dozen   B. 3 Dozen
    C. 25   D. 26

13. The largest digit number which is even and is a multiple of 3 is _____.
    A. 999   B. 102
    C. 888   D. 199

14. The sum of numbers from 1 to 12 is _____.
    A. 78   B. 59
    C. 73   D. 71

15. Rahul has 961 coins with her. Write 9671 in words.
    A. Seven hundred ninety six
    B. Seven hundred sixty nine
    C. Nine hundred seventy one
    D. Nine hundred sixty one

16. What is the face value of the underlined digit in the number given below
    38,_4_55.
    A. Four   B. Five
    C. Three   D. Eight

17. What is the expanded form of given number 12,554?
    A. 12 + 5 + 5 + 4
    B. 12,000 + 500 + 50 + 4
    C. 1200 + 54 + 5
    D. 1200 + 50 + 45

18. Find the greatest three digit number from the following ;
    341, 199, 111, 627, 245
    A. 341   B. 627
    C. 199   D. 245

19. Find the smallest three digit number from the following :
    341, 199, 111, 627, 245
    A. 627   B. 111
    C. 245   D. 199

20. Choose the correct option :
    A. 371 > 231   B. 591 < 326
    C. 140 > 200   D. 529 = 226

Direction (21-25) : In a group, there are 6 people i.e. grandfather, grandmother, father, mother, a boy and a girl. The age of the boy is 2 years. The girl is 3 years older than boy. Father's age is 7 times the age of the girl. Mother is three years younger than father. Grandfather's age is thirty times the age of the boy and grandmother is eleven times the age of the girl.

21. The age of grandmother is _____.
    A. 50 years   B. 55 years
    C. 60 years   D. 65 years

22. The difference between age of grandfather and grandmother is _____.
    A. 05 years   B. 10 years
    C. 15 years   D. None of these

23. Which of the following statement is true?
    A. Age of mother is 40 years
    B. Age of father is 48 years
    C. Grandfather is 18 years older than mot
    D. Age of father is 35 years

24. The age of grandfather is _____.
    A. 50 years   B. 55 years
    C. 60 years   D. 65 years

Unit–1 : Number System

25. How many members in the family are aged more than 43 but less than 65?
   A. 01
   B. 04
   C. 02
   D. 03

Direction (26-27): Consider the following numbers to answer the questions :

   4   17   9   45   22   19   12   34

26. If numbers are to be selected from the above list such that odd numbers are to be picked in ascending order, then what would be the sequence of numbers?
   A. 4, 12, 22, 34
   B. 9, 17, 19, 45
   C. 34, 22, 12, 4
   D. 45, 19, 17, 9

27. If numbers are to be selected from the above list such that even numbers are to be picked in descending order, then what would be the sequence of numbers?
   A. 4, 12, 22, 34
   B. 9, 17, 19, 45
   C. 34, 22, 12, 4
   D. 45, 19, 17, 9

Consider the following scenario to answer Questions (28-32):

In a class in year 2011, there were 55 students out of which 30 are girls. Two more new boys joined the class from 2012.

28. The total numbers of boys in the class in 2012 were _____.
   A. 20
   B. 30
   C. 27
   D. 55

29. The total numbers of boys in the class in 2011 were _____.
   A. 22
   B. 25
   C. 27
   D. 55

30. What was the strength of the class in 2011?
   A. 50
   B. 85
   C. 65
   D. 55

31. In year 2013, 3 girls leave and 1 more boy joined the class. What will be the strength of the class in 2013?
   A. 57
   B. 55
   C. 58
   D. 61

32. The total numbers of girls in the class in year 2013 are _____.
   A. 27
   B. 30
   A. 40
   B. 25

Answer Key

1. A	2. A	3. B	4. A	5. C	6. B	7. C	8. D
9. A	10. B	11. D	12. B	13. B	14. A	15. D	16. A
17. B	18. B	19. B	20. A	21. B	22. A	23. D	24. C
25. C	26. B	27. C	28. C	29. B	30. D	31. B	32. A

Hints and Solutions

1. Clearly 3116 is the smallest number.
2. Place value of 8 in 978353 is 8 × 1000 = 8000
3. We see that 946 > 853.
4. We know the sum of two even numbers is always an even number.
5. Hundreds place
6. ∵ 550 is divisible by 2. Hence 550 is an even number.
7. Here
   (1) 7000 + 400 + 20 + 6 = 7426
   (2) 7000 + 400 + 00 + 6 = 7406
   (3) 700 + 60 + 6 = 766
   (4) 7000 + 000 + 60 + 7 = 7067
8. Mangoes obtained by Vijay
   = 20 − (5 + 6)
   = 20 − 11 = 9
9. We know that the largest 3 digit number is 999.
10. 5 is an odd number.
11. Total number of fruits in the box
    $= 2 \times 12 + 2 + 1 + \dfrac{12}{2}$
    = 24 + 2 + 1 + 6 = 33
12. If three more bananas are added to box then the total number of fruits
    = 33 + 3 = 36
    = 3 × 12 = 3 dozen
13. ∵ 102 is an even number and $\dfrac{102}{3} = 34$
14. Required sum = 1 + 2 + 3 + 4 + 5 + 6 + 7 + 8 + 9 + 10 + 11 + 12 = 78
15. 961 — Nine hundred sixty one
16. Face value of 4 in 38, 455 = 4
17. We have 12554
    = 12000 + 500 + 50 + 4
18. Here 627 is the greatest three digit number
19. Here 111 is the smallest three digit number
20. Here 371 > 231.
    Solution 21– 236.
    Given age of the boy = 2 years
    Age of girl = 2 + 3 = 5 years
    Father's age = 7 × 5 = 35 years
    Mother's age = 35 − 3 = 32 years
    Grandfather's age = 30 × 2 = 60 years
21. Grandmother's age = 11 × 5
    = 55 years
22. Required difference = 60 − 55
    = 05 years
23. Age of father is 35 years
24. The age of grandfather = 60 years
25. There are 2 such persons.
26. Odd numbers are 17, 9, 45, 19
    ∵ Required ascending order is
    9, 17, 19, 45
27. Even numbers are = 4, 22, 12, 34
    ∵ Required in descending order is
    34, 22, 12, 4
28. Total numbers of boys in 2012
    = 55 − 30 + 2
    = 25 + 2 = 27 boys
29. Total numbers of boys in 2011
    = 25 boys
30. Total strength of the class in 2011 = 55
31. Strength of the class in 2013
    = 55 + 2 + 1 − 3 = 55
32. Total numbers of girls in the class in 2013 = 30 − 3 = 27

Unit-1 : Number System

Unit - 2 : Addition

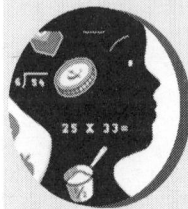

Learning Objectives : In this unit we, will learn about:
- Addition
- Addition of Four Digit Numbers
- Properties of Addition

Addition

Putting things together is called addition.
The numbers that are added are called addends. The result of addition is called the sum. It's sign is '+'.

Example :

```
15  +  17  =  32
 ↑      ↑      ↓
Addition      Sum
```

Put the given numbers at their correct places and always start adding from ones digits.

16   International MATHEMATICS Olympiad – Class 3

Addition of Four Digit Numbers

Example : Add 3425 and 2246.
Solution : Arranging the digits of the numbers 3425 and 2246 in column form.

Thousands Hundreds Tens Ones

```
  3      4     2   5
+ 2      2     4   4
_____
  5      6     6   9
```

Adding ones = 5 + 4 = 9 ones
Adding tens = 2 + 4 = 6 tens
Adding hundreds = 4 + 2 = 6 hundreds
Adding thousands = 3 + 2 = 5 thousands
Hence 3425 + 2244 = 5669

Properties of Addition

(i) If we change the order of numbers then the sum remains the same.
Example : 15 + 17 = 32 = 17 + 15
(ii) When we add 0 to any number the sum is the number itself.
Example : 20 + 0 = 20
(iii) The sum of three numbers is the same even if we change the grouping of the numbers.

Unit – 2 : Addition

Multiple Choice Questions

1. Find the missing digit.
   440 + _____ = 766
   A. 321
   B. 322
   C. 320
   D. 326

2. Find the missing digit.
   349 + 4 * 6 = 805
   A. 2
   B. 3
   C. 5
   D. 6

3. Find the missing number.
   A. 380
   B. 390
   C. 392
   D. 381

4. 7000 : 8000 : : 4000 : ___ ?
   A. 3000
   B. 4500
   C. 5000
   D. 8000

5. Find the next number.
   344, 351, 358, ____ , _____.
   A. 366
   B. 365
   C. 36
   D. 364, 371

6. Which number makes the equation true?
   ? + 1323 = 1223 + 1223
   A. 1223
   B. 1123
   C. 1213
   D. 1133

7. Which number makes the equation true?
   1508 + 125 = 2407 + ?
   A. 226
   B. 774
   C. 126
   D. – 774

8. Which number makes the equation true?
   20 + 30 = 15 + ?
   A. 25
   B. 40
   C. 30
   D. 35

9. Which options complete the pattern?
   4 + 5 = _____
   40 + 50 = _____
   400 + 500 = _____
   A. 9, 90, 900
   B. 9, 99,990
   C. 9,90, 990
   D. 9, 99, 900

10. Which numbers complete the pattern?
    _____ + 6 = 9
    _____ + 60 = 90
    _____ + 600 = 900
    A. 2, 22, 200
    B. 2, 20, 220
    C. 2, 22, 220
    D. 3, 30, 300

11. Look at the table below. What is rule for the table?

Input	Output
623	636
544	557
388	401
279	292

    A. Add 22
    B. Add 23
    C. Add 13
    D. Add 12

12. State whether the following statements are true or false
    A. 5746 + 2222 is as same as 3984 + 3984
    B. If we add 777 to 7777 we will get 8554

Unit - 2 : Additon

C. If we add 89 to 6789 we will get 6879

D. 3000 + 175 is more than 2981 + 179

A. TTFF   B. FFTT
C. TFTF   D. FTFT

13. State whether the following statements are true or false
    A. 6896 + 3583 = 10478
    B. If we add 333 + 4444 we will get 5777
    C. If we add 5432 and 1234 we will get 5555
    D. 2222 + 1357 = 3579
    A. TTFF   B. FTFT
    C. FFTT   D. TFTF

14. Ajay is 25 years old. His brother Vijay is 4 years elder to him. How old is Vijay?
    A. 21 years   B. 29 years
    C. 22 years   D. 24 years

15. Raju has 40 apples in a box. Ajay has 78 apples in another box. How many apples do Raju and Ajay have in all?
    A. 109   B. 118
    C. 119   D. 108

16. Viksha drive 140 km on Monday and 340 km on Tuesday. How many Kilometers did she drive in all?
    A. 470 km   B. 480 km
    C. 485 km   D. 475 km

17. Manoj works as mechanic at a service station. He repaired 150 cars and 190 motorcycles in 6 months. How many vehicles did Manoj repair in all?

A. 317   B. 217
C. 307   D. 340

18. Pooja is 40 years old. Pooja is 30 years old. If Ajay's age is equal to the sum of Kamla and Ajay age. How old is Ajay?
    A. 60 years   B. 90 years
    C. 80 years   D. 70 years

19. Class 2 students of a school go for a trip. The teacher takes 15 girls and 35 boys to a museum. How many tickets will they need to buy?
    A. 47 tickets   B. 48 tickets
    C. 49 tickets   D. 50 tickets

20. Shraddha, Ashima and Sonia bought some books. Sonia bought 10 books. Shraddha bought 5 more than Sonia. Ashima bought 3 more books than Shraddha. How many books did they buy in all?
    A. 15 books
    B. 40 books
    C. 43 books
    D. 18 books

Direction (21-24) : There are 1639 men, 1884 women, and 4230 Children in a village.

21. What is the total population of the village?
    A. 7763   B. 7700
    C. 7736   D. 7100

22. A factory moves 3638, 3709 and 2185 Soap – cakes in three days. How many soap – cakes does the factory move in three days?
    A. 9500   B. 9532
    C. 9541   D. 3700

Unit – 2 : Addition

23. There are 2592 goats, 1789 cows, and 3889 buffaloes in a town. How many cattle eve there in town?
   A. 8270
   B. 8200
   C. 8250
   D. 8300

24. There are 4879 male and 4729 female primary teachers in a state. What is the total no. of teachers in the state?
   A. 6900
   B. 9608
   C. 9500
   D. 8800

Direction (25-26) : The cost of a cooler is 3400 rupees and the cast of a almirah is 1875 rupees more than that of the cooler.

25. Find the cost of the almirah
   A. ₹ 5325
   B. ₹ 5300
   C. ₹ 5200
   D. ₹ 5250

26. Find the total cost of both the cooler and the almirah.
   A. ₹ 8500
   B. ₹ 8700
   C. ₹ 8775
   D. ₹ 8200

Answer Key

1. D	2. C	3. C	4. C	5. B	6. B	7. D	8. D
9. A	10. D	11. C	12. D	13. C	14. B	15. B	16. B
17. D	18. D	19. D	20. C	21. A	22. B	23. A	24. B
25. A	26. C						

Hints and Solutions

1. Missing digit = 766 − 440 = 326
2. Putting 's 5 in Place of * we see that
 349 + 456 = 805
3. Clearly 488 − 456 = 32
 ∴ ? = 360 + 32 = 392
4. Here 8000 − 7000 = 1000 then
 ? = 4000 + 1000 = 5000
5. The given series is
 344 $\xrightarrow{+7}$ 351 $\xrightarrow{+7}$ 358 $\xrightarrow{+7}$ 365
6. Since 1223 + 1223 = 2446
 Then ? = 2446 − 1323 = 1123
7. Here 125 + 1508 = 1633
 ∴ ? = 2407 − 1633 = 774
8. (D) 35
9. We see
 4 + 5 = 9
 40 + 50 = 90
 400 + 500 = 900
 40000 + 50000 = 90000
10. (D)
11. Add 13
12. (A) 5746 + 2222 = 7968 and
 3984 + 3984 = 7978 (False)
 (B) 777 + 7777 = 8554 (True)
 (C) 89 + 6789 = 6878 (False)
 (D) 3000 + 175 = 3175 and
 2981 + 179 = 3160 (False)
13. (D)
14. Vijay age = 25 + 4 = 29 years
15. Total no. of apples = 40 + 78 = 118
16. Total distance = 340 + 140 = 480 km
17. Total no. of vehicles = 150 + 190
 = 340
18. Ajay's age = 40 + 30 = 70 years
19. Total no. of tickets = 15 + 35 = 50
20. Total no. of books = 10 + 10 + 5 + 10 + 5 + 3 = 10 + 15 + 18 = 43
21. Total population of village
 = 1639 + 1894 + 4230 = 7763
22. Total no. of soap – cakes in 3 days
 = 3638 + 3709 + 2185 = 9532
23. Total no. of cattle in town
 = 2592 + 1789 + 3889 = 8270
24. Total no. of teachers in the state
 = 4879 + 4729 = 9608
25. Cast of almirah = 3450 + 1875
 = ₹ 5325
26. Total cost of cooler and almirah
 = 5325 + 3450 = ₹ 8775

Unit - 3 : Subtraction

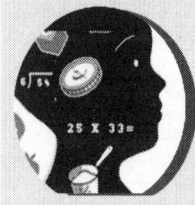

Learning Objectives : In this unit, we will learn about:

- Subtraction
- Subtraction of Four Digit Numbers
- Properties of Subtraction

Subtraction

Taking away some numbers from a group is called subtraction.

The number from which me subtract is called minuend and the number that is subtracted is called subtrahend. The value of subtraction is called difference. Subtraction is denoted by the symbol '–'.

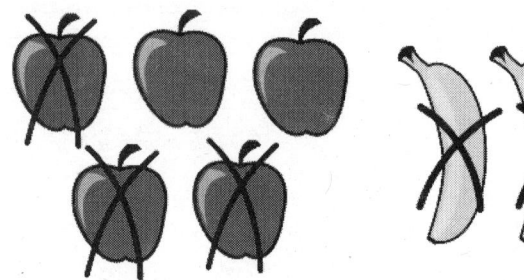

5 - 3 = 2 3 - 4 = -1

8874	–	4671	=	4203
↓		↓		↓
minuend		Subtrahend		difference

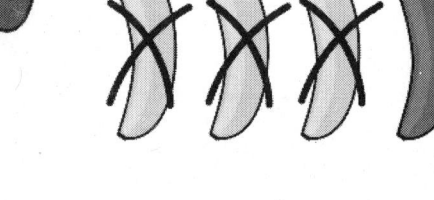

Hence 8874 – 4671 = 4203

Subtraction of Four Digit Numbers

Example : Subtract 4671 from 8874.

Solution : We have

Thousands	Hundreds	Tens	Ones
8	8	7	4
4	6	7	1
4	2	0	3

Subtracting ones   = 4 – 1 = 3
Subtracting tens   = 7 – 7 = 0
Subtracting hundreds = 8 – 6 = 2
Subtracting thousands = 8 – 4 = 4

Note : To check the answer, we add the smaller of the two given numbers to the answer and if the sum thus obtained is equal to the larger given number we say the answer is correct.

Properties of Subtraction

(i) When we subtract a numbers from itself, the difference is always zero
   Example : 24 – 24 = 0,   35 – 35 = 0
(ii) When we subtract zero from any number difference is the numbers itself.
   Example : 30 – 0 = 30,   21 – 0 = 21

Put the given numbers at their correct places and always subtract from ones digits.

Multiple Choice Questions

1. Find the missing digit.

    5? − 21 = 34

    A. 3 B. 4
    C. 5 D. 6

2. Find the missing digit.

    906 − 5?5 = 341

    A. 3 B. 4
    C. 5 D. 6

3. Find the missing number.

    670 : 630 : : 140 : ?

    A. 150 B. 180
    C. 90   D. 50

4. Find the missing number.

    250 : 100 : : ? : 200

    A. 260 B. 110
    C. 210 D. 350

5. Find the missing number

    340, 310, _____, 250

    A. 280 B. 210
    C. 270 D. 270

6. Which number makes the equation true?

    ? − 356 = 888 − 555

    A. 689 B. 333
    C. 889 D. 779

7. Which number makes the equation true?

    200 − 150 = 678 − ?

    A. 628 B. 528
    C. 523 D. 623

8. Which number makes the equation true ?

    66 − ? = 80 − 32

    A. 68 B. 48
    C. 58 D. 18

9. Which number complete the pattern?

    6 − 5 = ------

    60 − 50 = ------

    600 − 500 = ------

    6000 − 5000 = ------

    A. 1, 11, 111, 1111
    B. 1, 10, 100, 1000
    C. 11, 110, 111
    D. 10, 110, 111

10. Which number complete the pattern?

    9 − 5 = ------

    90 − 50 = ------

    900 − 500 = ------

    A. 4, 40, 440
    B. 5, 500, 550
    C. 5, 50, 500
    D. 5, 55, 550

11. Look at the table below. What is rule for the table?

Input	Output
345	331
456	442
789	775
910	896

International Mathematics Olympiad − Class 3

A. Subtract 10
B. Subtract 14
C. Subtract 16
D. Subtract 25

12. Look at the table. What is the rule for the table ?

Input	Output
300	330
200	230
100	130
400	430

A. Add 30   B. add 15
C. add 20   D. add 25

13. A book shop sold 50 books on Tuesday. It was 20 more than the number of book sold on Monday. How many were sold on Monday?
    A. 45 books   B. 30 books
    C. 65 books   D. 55 books

14. Vishal and Amit wrote a total of 678 words. If Vishal wrote 250 words, how many words did Amit write?
    A. 425 words   B. 428 words
    C. 931 words   D. 831 words

15. Shraddha painted 87 pots blue. This is 30 more than the number of red pots she painted. How many pots did Shraddha paint red?
    A. 116   B. 57
    C. 106   D. 48

16. In a bag, there are green and yellow balls. The bag has total of 800 balls out of which 420 are green. How many yellow balls are there in the bag?
    A. 259   B. 380
    C. 369   D. 269

17. There are 725 books in a book shop. On a particular day there was a sale of 125 books. How many books are there in the shop?
    A. 600   B. 699
    C. 599   D. 589

18. There are 600 students in a preschool. On a particular day, 450 students agreed to go for a field trip. How many students did not agree to go?
    A. 978   B. 150
    C. 222   D. 122

19. Pooja and Kamala have 34 stamps each. Pooja gives 10 stamps to Kamala. What is the difference between their stamps now?
    A. 20 stamps   B. 24 stamps
    C. 10 stamps   D. 25 stamps

20. Find the missing numbers.
    _____, 650, 635, 620, _____
    A. 665, 595   B. 675, 595
    C. 665, 605   D. 675, 605

Unit – 3 : Subtraction

Answer Key

1. C	2. D	3. B	4. D	5. A	6. A	7. A	8. D
9. B	10. A	11. B	12. A	13. B	14. B	15. B	16. B
17. A	18. B	19. B	20. C				

Hints and Solutions

1. We have 5 ? − 21 = 34
   ∴ ? − 1 = 4
   ∴ ? = 1 + 4 = 5
2. (D)
3. (B)
4. (D)
5. The given series is
   340 $\xrightarrow{-30}$ 310 $\xrightarrow{-30}$ 280
6. Putting ? = 689 we see that
   689 − 356 = 333
7. (A)
8. (D)
9. (B)
   The given series is
   6 − 5, 60 − 50, 600 − 500, 6000 − 5000
   ∴ 1, 10,   100,   1000

13. Required no. of books on Monday
    = 50 − 20 = 30
14. Required no. of words = 678 − 250
    = 428
15. Required no. of pots = 87 − 30
    = 57
16. Yellow balls = 800 − 420
    = 380
17. Remaining books in the shop
    = 725 − 125 = 600
18. Required no. of students = 600 − 450
    = 150
19. Required difference = 34 − 10 = 24
20. The given series is
    665 $\xrightarrow{-15}$ 650 $\xrightarrow{-15}$ 635 $\xrightarrow{-15}$ 620 $\xrightarrow{-15}$ 605

Unit-4 : Multiplication

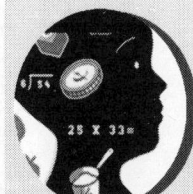

Learning Objectives : In this unit, we will learn about:
- Multiplication
- Multiplication of Four Digit Numbers
- Properties of Multiplication

Multiplication

We know that multiplication is repeated addition. The sign 'x' is used for multiplication. The number to be multiplied is called the multiplicand. The number by which another number is multiplied is called the multiplier. The result of multiplication is called product.

Multiplicand Multiplier Product
5 × 3 = 15

This is equivalent with
5 + 5 + 5 = 15

Example : This is a flower. It has 8 petals. How many petals are there in 5 such flowers?

Solution : Required number of petals
= 8 + 8 + 8 + 8 + 8 = 40, or 5 times 8 = 5 × 8 = 40

Example : This is an ant. It has 6 legs. How many legs do 7 ants have together?

Solution : Required no. of legs
= 6 + 6 + 6 + 6 + 6 + 6 + 6 = 42, or 7 times 6, or 7 x 6 = 42.

Example : This is a tray with Ladoos. It has 9 Ladoos. How many Ladoos are there in 6 trays?

Solution : Total number of Ladoos in 6 trays
= 9 + 9 + 9 + 9 + 9 + 9
= 54, or 6 times 9 = 54, or 6 x 9 = 54

Following table shows you a 12x12 grid for showing multiplication of all values of 12x12.

×	1	2	3	4	5	6	7	8	9	10	11	12
1	1	2	3	4	5	6	7	8	9	10	11	12
2	2	4	6	8	10	12	14	16	18	20	22	24
3	3	6	9	12	15	18	21	24	27	30	33	36
4	4	8	12	16	20	24	28	32	36	40	44	48
5	5	10	15	20	25	30	35	40	45	50	55	60
6	6	12	18	24	30	36	42	48	54	60	66	72
7	7	14	21	28	35	42	49	56	63	70	77	84
8	8	16	24	32	40	48	56	64	72	80	88	96
9	9	18	27	36	45	54	63	72	81	90	99	108
10	10	20	30	40	50	60	70	80	90	100	110	120
11	11	22	33	44	55	66	77	88	99	110	121	132
12	12	24	36	48	60	72	84	96	108	120	132	144

Multiplication of Four Digit Numbers

Example : Multiply 4342 by 2.

Solution : Thousands Hundreds Tens Ones

```
       4        3        4    2
                            ×  2
      ─────────────────────────
       8        6        8    4
```

2 ones × 2 = 4 ones
4 tens × 2 = 8 tens
3 hundreds × 2 = 6 hundreds
4 thousands × 2 = 8 thousands
Hence 4342 × 2 = 8684

Multiplication of 4 digit number by two digit number

Example: Multiply 22 × 12

```
Thousands Tens Ones
              2    2
    ×         1    2
    _____
    _____
```

Multiply the number by the ones digit 2, 22 × 2 ones = 44 ones
Write 44 in the first row

```
         4   4    Row I
  + 22   0        Row II
  _____
    26   4        Sum
```

Multiply the number by the tens digit 10.
    22 × 1 tens = 22 tens = 220
Write 220 in the second row.
Now add first and second rows.
Hence 22 × 12 = 264

Shortcut to problem solving

1. To write the table of 4, the trick to multiply the given number by 2 times.
   For example: 4 × 3 can be solved as 3 × 2 = 6 then 6 × 2 = 12, so 4 × 3 = 12.
2. If you know 6 × 5 = 30, then you can answer 5 × 6 = 30. If you know the answer to one of the facts then you can answer the other one too.
3. If you want to multiply any number with 10, just write '0' after that number.
   For example: 10 × 5 = 50
4. If you want to multiply any number with 11, just write number two times.
   For example: 11 × 7 = 77

Unit–4 : Multiplication

5. To multiply a number by 12, first multiply the number by 2 then add the two answers.

   For example : For 12 × 3, 3 × 2 = 6 and 3 × 10 = 30 so, 12 × 3 = 6 + 30 = 36.

   Hence 12 × 3 = 36.

Multiplication Table Trick

Let's say you want to write multiplication table of 29. Notice that the ten's digit is 2. The next higher number to 2 is 3.

So, the first part of each row will be previous row's ten's digit plus 3. And the last part of each row will be complement of that multiplier i.e. the unit place digit will be 9, 8, 7, 6, 5, 4, 3, 2, 1 & 0.

29 ×	1	= 2 / 9	= 29
29 ×	2	= (2 + 3) / 8	= 58
29 ×	3	= (5 + 3) / 7	= 87
29 ×	4	= (8 + 3) / 6	= 116
29 ×	5	= (11 + 3)/ 5	= 145
29 ×	6	= (14 + 3)/ 4	= 174
29 ×	7	= (17 + 3)/ 3	= 203
29 ×	8	= (20 + 3)/ 2	= 232
29 ×	9	= (23 + 3)/ 1	= 261
29 ×	10	= (26 + 3)/ 0	= 290

So, you saw the pattern? We can write any table, with digit 9 at unit place, by using this trick.

Example : Let us now see the table of 59.

The ten's digit here is 5. The next higher number to 5 is 6.

So, the first part of each row will be 6 plus previous answer's ten's digit. The last part of each row will be 9, 8, 7, 6, 5, 4, 3, 2, 1 & 0.

59 ×	1	= 5 / 9	= 59
59 ×	2	= (5 + 6) / 8	= 118
59 ×	3	= (11 + 6) / 7	= 177
59 ×	4	= (17 + 6) / 6	= 236
59 ×	5	= (23 + 6)/ 5	= 295
59 ×	6	= (29 + 6)/ 4	= 354
59 ×	7	= (35 + 6)/ 3	= 413
59 ×	8	= (41 + 6)/ 2	= 472
59 ×	9	= (47 + 6)/ 1	= 531
59 ×	10	= (53 + 6)/ 0	= 590

Properties of Multiplication

(i) The product of 0 and any number is 0.
   Example : $2 \times 0 = 0, 5 \times 0 = 0, 0 \times 99 = 0$

(ii) The product of 1 and any number is the number itself.
   Example : $3 \times 1 = 3, 1 \times 4 = 4, 99 \times 1 = 99$

(iii) The product of two of more numbers grouped in any order remains the same.

Examples :

$2 \times 4 \times 5 = (2 \times 4) \times 5 = 8 \times 5 = 40$
$2 \times 4 \times 5 = 2 \times (4 \times 5) = 2 \times 20 = 40$
$2 \times 4 \times 5 = (2 \times 5) \times 4 = 10 \times 4 = 40$

Unit-4 : Multiplication

Multiple Choice Questions

1. Find the missing

   3 x 6 : 6 x 3 : : 7 x 4 : ?

   A. 6 x 3   B. 7 x 3
   D. 4 x 7   D. 4 x 6

2. Pick the odd one out
   A. 2 x 13 = 36   B. 6 x 6 = 36
   C. 4 x 9 = 36   D. 12 x 3 = 36

3. Golu was checking his brother maths homework and found some facts different from the other. Find the odd one out:
   A. 17 x 5 = 85   B. 3 x 21 = 63
   C. 9 x 24 = 216   D. 18 x 6 = 104

4. For the above question, find the odd one out of the following:
   A. 9 x 13 = 13 + 13 + 13 + 13 + 13 + 13 + 13 + 13
   B. 15 x 6 = 90
   C. 23 x 2 = 23 + 23
   D. 7 x 14 = 7 + 7 + 7 + 7 + 7 + 7 + 7 + 7 + 7 + 7 + 7 + 7

5. 7 pens are put in a pen stand and there are 9 such pen stands. How many pens are there in all?
   A. 63   B. 64
   C. 65   D. 69

6. A basket has 10 apples in it. How many apples are there in 7 such baskets?
   A. 60   B. 70
   C. 80   D. 90

7. Ritu reads 26 page of a book in one day. How many pages can she read in 4 days?
   A. 100   B. 105
   C. 104   D. 108

8. 5 x 6 x 3 = ?
   A. 18   B. 15
   C. 30   D. 90

9. The number to be multiplied is called the _____.
   A. Multiplicand   B. Multiplier
   C. Product   D. None of these

10. The product of '0' and any number is _____.
    A. 1   B. 0
    C. Both of them   D. None of these

11. Choose the correct option.

    10 x -------- = 90

    A. 8   B. 9
    C. 19   D. 90

12. Choose the correct option.

    _____ x 9 = 36

    A. 4   B. 2
    C. 8   D. 7

13. Which one of the following statement is incorrect?

    Statement A : 12 pairs of socks are 24 socks.

    Statement B : 5 rainbows have 35 colors.

    Statement C : 8 dice have 45 faces.

    Statement D : 4 Tic-tac-toe games have 36 boxes.

    A. C   B. D
    C. A   D. B

14. Jojo multiplied 3 with a number and found an answer. His friend Jeenu made 9 groups of a number and found that his answer is same as Jojo answer so he shared it with her sister Juni. Juni told Jeenu that he has just interchanged the numbers multiplied by Jojo. Can you find the answer that both Jojo and Jeenu found?
    A. 30
    B. 29
    C. 28
    D. 27

Direction (15-18) : Mr Zambie collected different buttons and made a table to show his collections. Look at the table given below and answer the questions that follow.

S. No.	Color	Buttons
1	Red	3 boxes of 7 buttons
2	Green	8 boxes of 6 buttons
3	Blue	5 boxes of 9 buttons
4	Black	7 boxes of 10 buttons

15. How many black buttons are there?
    A. 70
    B. 71
    C. 72
    D. 73

16. How many red buttons were collected?
    A. 20
    B. 21
    C. 22
    D. 23

17. How many green buttons are shown in the table?
    A. 46
    B. 47
    C. 48
    D. 49

18. How many blue buttons are collected?
    A. 42
    B. 43
    C. 44
    D. 45

19. A car travels 75 km in one hour. How far will it travel in 9 hours ?
    A. 600 km
    B. 620 km
    C. 240 km
    D. 675 km

20. A train has 4 compartments. There are 72 passengers in each of them .How many passengers were there in the train?
    A. 250
    B. 266
    C. 272
    D. 288

Answer Key

1. C	2. A	3. D	4. D	5. A	6. B	7. C	8. D
9. A	10. B	11. B	12. A	13. A	14. D	15. A	16. B
17. C	18. D	19. D	20. D				

Unit - 4 : Multiplication

Unit - 5 : Division

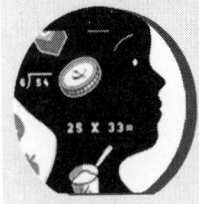

Learning Objectives : In this unit we will learn about:
- Division
- Opposite of Multiplication
- Division of Four Digit Numbers
- Properties of Division

Division

Division is a process of distribution equally among a group. Sharing and subtracting repeatedly are two of the basic ways of division. It is denoted by the symbol ' ÷ '. We use multiplication tables in dividing.

Example : There are 12 chocolates, and 3 friends want to share them, how do they divide the chocolates?

12 Chocolates

12 Chocolates Divided by 3

Answer : 12 divided by 3 is 4: they get 4 each.

Terms associated with Division

In division the number by which we divide is called the divisor, the number that we divide is called the dividend and the answer is the quotient. If there is a number left over, it is called the remainder.

Names

There are special names for each number in a division :

$$\text{Dividend} \div \text{Divisor} = \text{Quotient}$$

International Mathematics Olympiad - Class 3

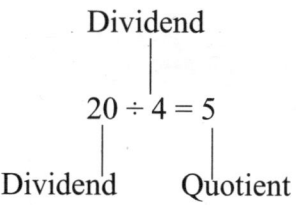

Example : In 24 ÷ 4 = 6
- 24 is the dividend
- 4 is the divisor
- 6 is the quotient

Opposite of Multiplication

Division and multiplication are inverse of each other. When we know a multiplication fact we can find its division fact:

Example : If 5 × 4 = 20 then division facts of 5 × 4 are 20 ÷ 5 = 4 and 20 ÷ 4 = 5
To know the reason for this consider given figure.

Example :

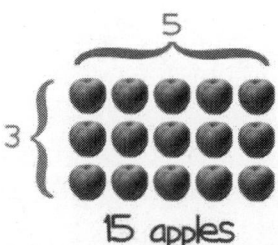

For the above figure, if we consider multiplication and division :

Multiplication	Division
3 groups of 5 make 15	So 15 divided by 3 is 5
5 groups of 3 make 15	So 15 divided by 5 is 3.

So there are **four related facts** :
- 3 × 5 = 15
- 5 × 3 = 15
- 15 / 3 = 5
- 15 / 5 = 3

Checking answer

Answer can be checked is the following methods :

$$\text{Quotient} \times \text{Divisor} + \text{Remainder} = \text{Dividend}$$

Unit – 5 : Division

Note : Knowing your Multiplication Tables(covered in Multiplication chapter) can help you with division.

Example : What is 28 ÷ 7?

If you go through the multiplication table we find that 28 is 4 × 7, so 28 divided by 7 must be 4.

X	1	2	3	4
1	1	2	3	4
2	2	4	6	8
3	3	6	9	12
4	4	8	12	16
5	5	10	15	20
6	6	12	18	24
7	7	14	21	28

Answer : 28 ÷ 7 = 4

Remainder

Sometimes we cannot divide things up evenly.

Example : There are 7 bones to share with 2 pups. But 7 cannot be divided exactly in 2 groups, so each pup gets 3 bones, but there will be 1 left over:

7 ÷ 2 = 3 R 1 ← Remainder

That 1 left over is called Remainder.

Things to Remember

1. If you make groups of 1 then the answer is number itself as any number divided by 1 is the number itself. For example, 4 ÷ 1 = 4, 12 ÷ 1 = 12 etc.
2. If the given number ends with 0 or 5 then you can divide the number in groups of 5. For example, 25 = 5 groups of 5 or 25 ÷ 5 = 5, 10 = 2 groups of 5 or 10 ÷ 5 = 2 etc.
3. If the given number ends with 0 then you can divide the number in groups of 10.
   Example : 40 = 4 groups of 10 or 40 ÷ 10 = 4, etc.
4. When any number is divided by zero, the answer is infinity.
   Example : 1234 ÷ 0 = Infinity.

Shortcuts

1. To divide any number by 5, multiply by 2 and divide by 10.
2. To divide any number by 25, multiply by 4 and divide by 100.

Division of Four Digit Numbers

Example : Divide 2514 by 6.

Solution :

∵ 2 < 6 it cannot be divided. Combine it with digit.

```
       419
   6 )2514
      24
      ――
      11
       6
      ――
       54
       54
      ――
        ×
```

Example : Divide 789 by 6.

Since 6 < 7 then we can not divide 7 by 6

```
      131
   6 )789
      6
     ――
     18
     18
     ――
       9
       6
      ――
       3
```

Here Quotient = 131
Remainder = 3
To check answer we use
  Dividend = Divisor × Quotient + Remainder
      789 = 6 × 131 + 3
Hence, the answer is correct.

Properties of Division

1) When 0 is divided by any number (other than 0) the quotient is zero.
    Example : $0 ÷ 2 = 0, 0 ÷ 5 = 0$

(ii) When any number is divided by 0 the quotient is infinitive (∞).
Example :
$$\left(\frac{1}{0} = \infty, \frac{5}{0} = \infty\right)$$

(iii) When a number is divided by 1, the quotient is the number itself.
Example :
$$\left(\frac{55}{1} = 55, \frac{799}{1} = 799\right)$$

(iv) When a number (other than 0) is divided by itself the quotient is 1.
Example :
$$\left(\frac{5}{5} = 1, \frac{4}{4} = 1, \frac{99}{99} = 1\right)$$

Multiple Choice Questions

1. 30 ÷ 5 = ?
   A. 5
   B. 6
   C. 4
   D. 10

2. 60 ÷ 10 = ?
   A. 10
   B. 6
   C. 4
   D. 16

3. If 3 × 4 = 12; 12 ÷ 4 = ?
   A. 3
   B. 4
   C. 12
   D. 6

4. If 1 × 3 = 3; 3 ÷ 3 = ?
   A. 3
   B. 9
   C. 6
   D. 1

5. If 6 × 8 = 48; 48 ÷ 8 = ?
   A. 5
   B. 4
   C. 6
   D. 8

6. 4 + 4 + 4 + 4 + 4 + 4 + 4 = 28

   There are 7 groups of number 4. Which is the correct way to write this?
   A. 4 × 28
   B. 28 ÷ 4
   C. 7 × 4
   D. 4 × 8

7. Which two pairs are same?
   A. 3 ÷ 3, 16 ÷ 2
   B. 10 ÷ 2, 12 ÷ 2
   C. 18 ÷ 3, 27 ÷ 3
   D. 4 ÷ 2, 6 ÷ 3

8. Any number divided by zero will give the answer as
   A. Zero
   B. One
   C. Infinity
   D. None of these

9. If the given number ends with 0, we can divide the numbers by:
   A. 10
   B. 2
   C. 3
   D. 0

10. 24 ÷ 6 : 2 groups of 2 :: 18 ÷ 2 : ?
    A. 2 groups of 2
    B. 3 groups of 3
    C. 2 groups of 3
    D. 3 groups of 2

11. 28 ÷ 4 : ? :: 16 ÷ 4 : 4
    A. 4
    B. 6
    C. 7
    D. 5

12. 10 ÷ 10 : 1 :: 100 ÷ 100 : ?
    A. 1
    B. 10
    C. 100
    D. None of thes

13. Which one of the following is correct?
    A. 7 × 7 = 56
    B. 8 × 7 = 54
    C. 56 ÷ 7 = 8
    D. 8 ÷ 56 = 7

14. Which one of the following is incorrect?
    A. 54 ÷ 6 = 9
    B. 9 ÷ 54 = 6
    C. 6 × 9 = 54
    D. 9 × 6 = 54

15. 20 apples are shared equally among six children. How many apples are left over?
    A. 4
    B. 3
    C. 2
    D. 1

16. 50 chocolates are shared equally among seven children. How many chocolates are left over?
    A. 1
    B. 2
    C. 3
    D. 4

17. Find the value of x

    24 ÷ 4 : 6 :: 28 ÷ 4 : x
    A. 5
    B. 6
    C. 7
    D. 8

Unit - 5 : Division

18. Pick the odd one out
    A. 2 groups of 6 is same as 12 ÷ 2
    B. 2 groups of 4 is same as 8 ÷ 2
    C. 2 groups of 7 is same as 14 ÷ 2
    D. 2 groups of 8 is same as 16 ÷ 2
    A. D   B. C
    C. A   D. B

19. Madhu bought 27 roses bundles and planted them evenly in 3 rows. How many rose bushes are in each row?
    A. 9   B. 8
    C. 27   D. 3

20. Shraddha clicked 24 pictures. She distributed them equally in 8 friends. How many picture does each friend has?
    A. 8   B. 4
    C. 3   D. 24

Direction (21-24) : Read the following passage and carefully answers the questions given below.
Shraddha has written same division facts in her math note book. She was amazed to see that all the answer are from 0 – 9. Answer the division facts given below using number 0 – 9 only.

21. 81 ÷ 9
    A. 6   B. 7
    C. 8   D. 9

22. 56 ÷ 7
    A. 6   B. 7
    C. 8   D. 9

23. 63 ÷ 9
    A. 6   B. 7
    C. 8   D. 9

24. 48 ÷ 8
    A. 6   B. 7
    C. 8   D. 9

25. 7 trucks can carry 455 boxes of apples. How many boxes can be carried by each truck ?
    A. 60   B. 65
    C. 70   D. 63

26. The number of students in a school is 9.8%. Find the number of students in each class if there are 8 classes and each has equal number of students.
    A. 124   B. 125
    C. 123   D. 126

27. The product of two numbers is 1224. If one of them is 6, find the other.
    A. 204   B. 200
    C. 102   D. 1300

28. A poultry farm produced 1743 eggs in a week. Find the number of eggs each day.
    A. 250   B. 251
    C. 200   D. 249

29. A shopkeeper bought some books each costing ₹ 9. He gave ₹ 7820 to the wholesaler. How many books did he buy and how many rupees did he get back ?
    A. 868, 7   B. 860, 8
    C. 868, 8   D. 868, 6

30. How many piees of 5 cm can be cut from a ribbon 85 cm in length?
    A. 17   B. 15
    C. 16   D. 18

Answer Key

1. B	2. B	3. A	4. D	5. C	6. C	7. D	8. C
9. A	10. B	11. C	12. A	13. C	14. B	15. C	16. A
17. C	18. A	19. A	20. C	21. D	22. C	23. B	24. A
25. B	26. C	27. A	28. D	29. C	30. A		

Hints and Solutions

13. $56 \div 7 = 8$ is the correct answer.
14. The correct answer is B. We can't divide 9 into 54 equal parts and get a whole number answer!
15. The correct answer is C.
    $\therefore 6 \times 3 = 18$, so each child gets 3 apples. The number of apples left over
    $= 20 - 18 = 2$ (2 is the remainder)
16. $7 \times 7 = 49$, so each child gets 7 chocolates. The number of chocolates left over $= 50 - 49 = 1$
    (In other words, 50 divided by 7 equals 7 with a remainder of 1)
25. Given 7 trucks can carry 455 boxes of apples
    $\therefore$ Required no. of boxes $= \dfrac{455}{7} = 65$
26. No. of students in school 984
    $\therefore$ No of students in each class
    $= \dfrac{984}{8} = 123$
27. If x is other number then
    $x = \dfrac{1224}{6} = 204$

28. There is seven days in a week.
    $\therefore$ No. of eggs produced in a day $= \dfrac{1743}{7}$
    $= 249$
29. Here

    $$\begin{array}{r} 868 \\ 9\overline{)7820} \\ 72 \\ \overline{62} \\ 54 \\ \overline{80} \\ 72 \\ \overline{8} \end{array}$$

    Clearly shopkeeper will buy 868 books
30. Given, total length of the ribbon
    $= 85$ cm
    Length of each piece $= 5$ cm
    $\therefore$ No of pieces that can be cut from the ribbon $= \dfrac{85}{5} = 17$

1. Choose the correct option to show the shaded part/fraction of the following figure.

Unit-5 : Division

Unit - 6 : Fractions

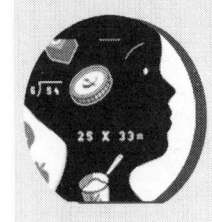

Learning Objectives : In this unit, we will learn about:
- Fraction
- Properties of fraction
- Equivalent fraction
- Types of fraction

Fraction
When a whole object is divided into equal parts, each part is called a fraction of that whole.

Suppose, there is a mango and you want to divide it equally among two friends then equal pieces of the mango form fractions. A fraction is a part of a whole divided into equal parts.

A fraction is written in the form of $\frac{N}{D}$; D ≠ 0. Here, N is called numerator and D is called the denominator. For example, $\frac{1}{3}$ means one part out of 3 equal parts.

Properties of Fraction
We often hear terms like half, one fourth and three fourth.

Halves
When a whole objeet is divided into two equal parts, each of the part is called one half of the whole object. One-half is written as $\frac{1}{2}$. It is read as one by two or one over two – equal parts.

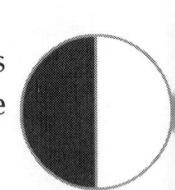

Quarters
When a whole object is divided into four equal parts, each of the part is called a quarter or one-fourth of the whole object. Quarter or one-fourth of the whole object. It is read as one by four or one over four and is written as $\frac{1}{4}$.

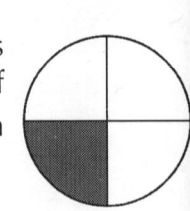

Thirds

When a whole object is divided into three equal parts, each of these part is called one third of the whole. It is written as $\frac{1}{3}$. It is read as one by three or one over three.

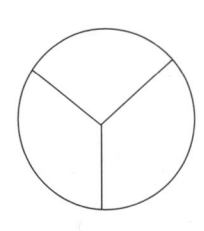

Equal or Equivalent Fractions

Fractions that appear differently but have the same value are equivalent fractions. For example, following values in the figures are equivalent:

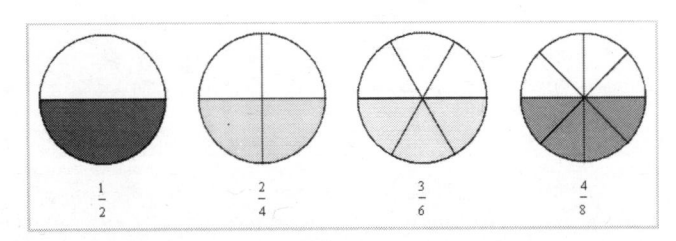

$$\frac{1}{2} \quad \frac{2}{4} \quad \frac{3}{6} \quad \frac{4}{8}$$

Rules to get equivalent fractions

(i) In a fraction, multiply the numerator and denominator by the same number (except 0) to get an equivalent fraction.

For example, $\frac{1}{4} = \frac{1}{4} \times \frac{3}{3} = \frac{3}{12}$

So, $\frac{1}{4}$ and $\frac{3}{12}$ are equivalent fractions.

(ii) We can also get a fraction equivalent to a given fraction dividing its numerator and denominator by the same numeral (except zero).

For example, $\frac{3 \div 3}{6 \div 3} = \frac{1}{2}$

Types of fractions

Let us check out different types of fractions with example

(i) Like Fractions

Fractions with same denominators are called like fractions.

For example: $\frac{1}{4}, \frac{3}{4}, \frac{5}{4}$ are like fractions.

(ii) Unlike Fractions

Fractions with different denominators are called unlike fractions.

For example : $\frac{1}{2}, \frac{1}{3}, \frac{1}{5}$ are unlike fractions.

Unit-6 : Fractions

(iii) Proper fractions
The numerator is less than the denominator as shown in following examples :

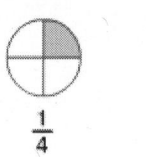

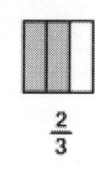

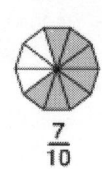

$\frac{1}{4}$ $\frac{2}{3}$ $\frac{7}{10}$

(iv) Improper fractions
The numerator is greater than the denominator as shown in following examples:

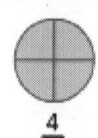

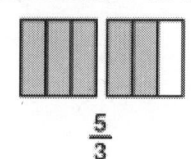

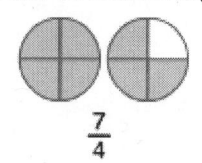

$\frac{4}{4}$ $\frac{5}{3}$ $\frac{7}{4}$

(v) Mixed fractions
A number written as a whole number with a prope fraction as shown in following examples:

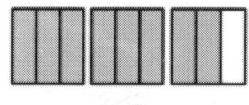

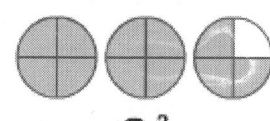

$2\frac{2}{3}$ $2\frac{3}{4}$

Did You Know?
Our body is composed of an average $\frac{3}{5}$ th part of water.

Note on Equivalent Fractional Numbers
Two fractions are equivalent if the product of the numerators of the first fraction and the denominator of the second fraction is equal to the product of the denominator of the first fraction and the numerator of second and fraction.

Multiple Choice Questions

1. Choose the correct option to show the shaded part/fraction of the following figure.

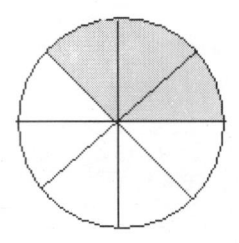

   A. 3/8 B. 8/3
   C. 1/8 D. 1/2

2. Which figure is shaded to show a fraction equal to 2/5 of its whole?

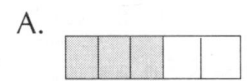

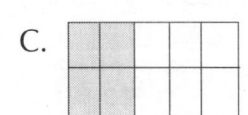

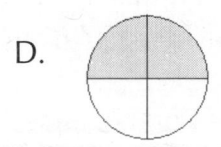

   A.
   B.
   C.
   D.

3. Which two fractions are equivalent?
   A. 1/2 and 1/3
   B. 1/2 and 2/4
   C. 1/4 and 1/6
   D. 2/3 and 1/3

4. The figures below show that .

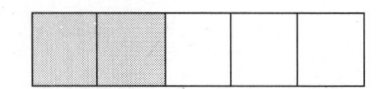

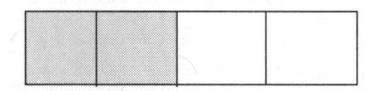

   A. 1/5 = 1/4 B. 2/5 = 2/4
   C. 2/5 > 2/4 D. 2/5 < 2/4

5. Half of half is the same as the fraction:
   A. 1/2 B. 1/4
   C. 2/4 D. 3/4

6. If the fractions N/6 and 2/3 are equivalent, what is the value of N?
   A. N = 2 B. N = 1
   C. N = 4 D. N = 3

Unit-5 : Division

7. Which two figures have shaded parts that represent equivalent fractions?

A.

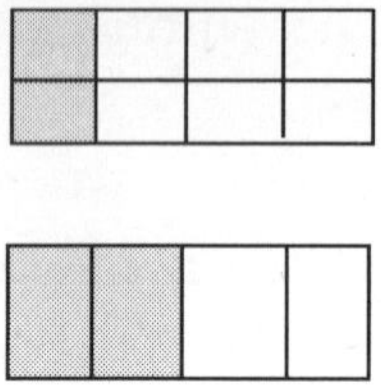

B.

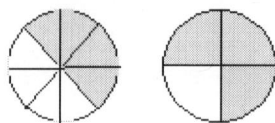

C.

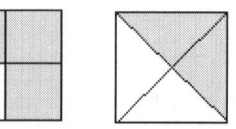

D.

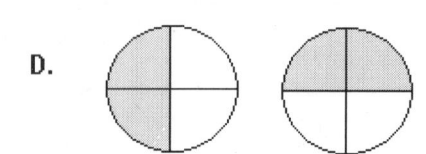

8. Order from greatest to least the fractions **1/3 , 1/6 , 1/2 , 1/7**.
   A. 1/2 , 1/3 , 1/6 , 1/7
   B. 1/7 , 1/6 , 1/3 , 1/2
   C. 1/2 , 1/6 , 1/3 , 1/7
   D. 1/7 , 1/2 , 1/3 , 1/6

9. What value of the number N given below makes **N/3 < 1/2**?
   A. N = 3   B. N = 2
   C. N = 1   D. N = 4

10. Shraddha, Ashima, Swati and Priya bought 2 pizzas of the same size. Shraddha ate 2/4 of a pizza. Ashima, Swati and Priya ate 1/4 of a pizza each. How much pizza was left?
    A. 1/4 of a pizza   B. 1 pizza
    C. 1/2 of a pizza   D. 3/4 of a pizza

11. $\frac{1}{4} : \frac{2}{8} :: \frac{1}{3} : ?$
    A. $\frac{3}{6}$ B. $\frac{2}{6}$
    C. $\frac{3}{9}$ D. $\frac{2}{3}$

12. $\frac{3}{4} : \frac{4}{3} :: \frac{2}{5} : ?$
    A. $\frac{5}{2}$ B. $\frac{2}{10}$
    C. $\frac{5}{10}$ D. $\frac{3}{10}$

13. $\frac{1}{2} : \frac{1}{4} :: \frac{1}{5} : ?$
    A. $\frac{1}{8}$ B. $\frac{1}{10}$
    C. $\frac{1}{15}$ D. $\frac{1}{6}$

14. Golu, Ankit and Ashu bought an apple they wanted to share the apple equally. They cut the apple in three equal parts. Which of the following statements are true?
    i. They all get 1/3 of the apple
    ii. Ankit gets a smaller part than Ashu
    iii. Golu gets one-third of the apple
    iv. Ankit gets one-fourth of the apple
    A. TTFF   B. TTTF
    C. FFFT   D. TFTF

15. How many hours are in ½ of a day?
    A. 6 hours
    B. 12 hours
    C. 18 hours
    D. 10 hours

16. How many months are in ¼ of an year?
    A. 2 months
    B. 4 months
    C. 3 months
    D. 6 months

17. Shraddha had 5 blue balls in a bag. She put 3 more red ball in the bag. What fraction of the balls were red?
    A. 3/5
    B. 3/8
    C. 2/5
    D. 5/8

18. There are 12 people standing in a queue at a ticket counter. One-fourth of the people in the queue are women. How many women are standing?
    A. 3 women
    B. 4 women
    C. 2 women
    D. 6 women

19. There are 10 birds on a branch of tree. One-fifth of the birds flew away. How many birds are left on the branch?
    A. 5 birds
    B. 2 birds
    C. 8 birds
    D. 6 birds

20. Shubhra got 4 pastries. She served 2 of them to the guests and kept the remaining in the refrigerator. What fraction of pastries are kept in refrigerator?
    A. ¼
    B. ¾
    C. ⅓
    D. ½

Answer Key

1. A	2. C	3. B	4. D	5. B	6. C	7. D	8. A
9. C	10. D	11. B	12. A	13. B	14. D	15. B	16. C
17. B	18. A	19. C	20. D				

Unit – 5 : Division

47

Hints and Solutions

2. We have $\dfrac{4}{10} = \dfrac{2}{5}$

3. Have $\dfrac{1}{2}$ and $\dfrac{2}{5} = \dfrac{1}{2}$. Clearly they are equivalent.

4. From figure (i) $\dfrac{1}{2}$ and from (ii) $\dfrac{2}{4} = \dfrac{1}{2}$

   Clearly $\dfrac{2}{5} < \dfrac{1}{4}$

5. We have Half of Half means $\dfrac{1}{2}$ of $\dfrac{1}{2}$

   $= \dfrac{1}{4}$

6. Given $\dfrac{N}{6}$ and $\dfrac{2}{3}$ are equivalent

   $\therefore \dfrac{N}{6} = \dfrac{2}{3}$ is $N = 6 \times \dfrac{2}{3} = 4$

8. Here LCM of 3, 6, 2 and 7 is 42

   $\therefore \dfrac{1}{3}, \dfrac{1}{6}, \dfrac{1}{2}, \dfrac{1}{7} = \dfrac{14}{42}, \dfrac{7}{42}, \dfrac{21}{42}, \dfrac{6}{42}$

   $\therefore$ Correct order is $\dfrac{21}{42}, \dfrac{14}{42}, \dfrac{7}{42}, \dfrac{6}{42}$

   $= \dfrac{1}{2}, \dfrac{1}{3}, \dfrac{1}{6}$ and $\dfrac{1}{7}$

10. Required pizza $= 2 - \dfrac{2}{4} + \dfrac{3}{4} = 2 - \dfrac{5}{4}$

    $= \dfrac{8-5}{4}$

    $= \dfrac{3}{4}$ of a pizza

11. Here $\dfrac{1}{4} : \dfrac{2}{8} :: \dfrac{1}{3} : ?$

    $\therefore \dfrac{1}{4} = \dfrac{2}{2} \times \dfrac{1}{4} = \dfrac{2}{8}$ then ?

    $= \dfrac{2 \times 1}{2 \times 3} = \dfrac{2}{6}$

12. $\because \dfrac{3}{4} = \dfrac{1}{3/4} = \dfrac{4}{3}$ then ? $= \dfrac{1}{2/5} = \dfrac{5}{2}$

13. $\dfrac{1}{2} : \dfrac{1}{4} :: \dfrac{1}{5} : ? \Rightarrow ? = \dfrac{1}{2 \times 5} = \dfrac{1}{10}$

15. Required hours in a day $= \dfrac{24}{2}$

    $= 12$ hours

20. Required fraction $= \dfrac{2}{4} = \dfrac{1}{2}$

Unit - 7 : Length

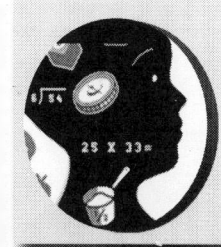

Learning Objectives : In this unit, we will learn about:
- Length
- Measuring Tapes

Length

Measurement of length helps us in knowing the distance between two points. The standard unit of length is metre (m).

Rulers are used to measure small objects. We measure length in terms of standard units of meter, decimeter and centimeter. Pencil, nail, dipper, etc. can be measured in centimeters.

We can measure the length of the pencil using a ruler.

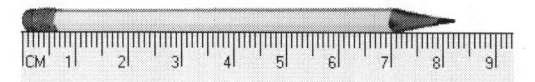

Measuring Tapes

Measuring tapes are used to measure large objects. cloth, rope etc are measured in meters. Measuring tapes are also used to measure body parts.

We need a bigger unit of length to measure the distance between two towns, the length of a road. For these purpose, we use the unit kilometer.

$$1 \text{ km} = 1000 \text{ meter}$$

Measurement using rulers or Measuring tapes

(i) Place one end of the item with '0'in the ruler/measuring tapes.
(ii) Both the items and the ruler/measuring tapes should be straight.
(iii) Start reading the scale on ruler/measuring tapes.
(iv) Stop reading the scale where the item ends.
(v) Hold the last end of the item and read the scale

Relation between meter, decimeter and centimeter

Centimeter to meter
1. 100 centimeter (cm) = 1 meter (m)
    Centimeter to decimeter
2. 10 centimeter (cm) = 1 decimeter (dm)
    Decimeter to meter
3. 10 decimeter (dm) = 1 meter(m)

Conversion

(i) To convert 'm' into 'cm' we multiply the numbers by 100.
(ii) To convert 'm' into 'cm' we divide the numbers by 100.

Misconcept/Concept

Misconcept : Some large rulers can measure long distances.

Concept : Rulers cannot be used to measure long distances irrespective of how big the ruler be. A ruler cannot be used to measure unit such as kilometers.

Multiple Choice Questions

1. Golu wants to measure the length of a cloth. Which measuring instrument among the following he should use to measure the cloth?
   A. Ruler B. Hand
   C. Meter rod D. Foot

2. Ankit want to measure the length of different things. Match the measuring things given in list I with the measuring instrument given in the list II to help Ankit find the length of the items.

	List I		List II
A.	Length of a kurta	1.	Ruler
B.	Length of a Book	2.	Foot
C.	Length of a Dupatta	3.	Measuring Tape
D.	Length of a Carpet	4.	Metre rod

	A	B	C	D
A.	3	2	1	4
B.	4	1	3	2
C.	2	4	3	1
D.	3	1	4	2

3. Choose the correct option to replace the question mark.
   Ruler : Centimeter :: Measuring Tape : ?
   A. Centimeter B. Meter
   C. Millimeter D. Kilometer

4. Find the missing
   Distance from one house to next house : Meters :: Distance from house to school : ?
   A. Centimeters B. Meters
   C. Millimeters D. Kilometers

Direction (5-7) : Gaurav Singh is a Tailor. He uses different lengths of cloth to make dresses for girls. He prepared a table for the length of cloth needed for each dress he makes. Read the table given below and answer the questions that follows:

S. No.	Name of the dress	Length of cloth required
1.	Frock	4 meters
2.	Skirt	3 meters
3.	Shorts	125 centimeters
4.	Kurti	250 centimeters
5.	Jeans	2 meters

5. Which dress require maximum length of cloth?
   A. Frock B. Skirt
   C. Shorts D. Kurti

6. Which dress requires minimum length of cloth?
   A. Skirt B. Shorts
   C. Kurti D. Jeans

7. Which of the following statement is incorrect.?
   A: Kurti needs more cloth than jeans.
   B: Shorts needs more cloth than skirt.
   C: Frock needs more cloth than skirt.
   D: Jeans needs less cloth than frock.
   A. B B. C
   C. D D. A

8. Things which can be in centimeters
   A. Length of banana
   B. Height of a water bottle

Unit – 7 : Length

C. Width of T.V.
D. Length of kurta

9. Things which will be in meters.
   A. Depth of a pond
   B. Height of a tree
   C. Height of a cat
   D. Distance in a room

Directions (10-18) : Choose the correct option from the following :

10. The standard unit of length is ———.
    A. A meter   B. Hundred
    C. 15cm   D. 15cm scale

11. Cloth merchant use a —— to measure cloths.
    A. Hockey stick   B. Meter rod
    C. Cricket bat   D. 15cm scale

12. To measure small length we use a ——
    A. Banana   B. Hand
    C. 15cm   D. A pen

13. 1 meter has —— cms
    A. Thousand   B. Ten
    C. Ten thousands D. Hundred

14. 1 decimeter has —— centimeters.
    A. 10   B. 50
    C. 100   D. 1000

15. A 15-centimeter scale can measure length upto ——
    A. 20cm   B. 15cm
    C. 25cm   D. 10cm

16. Suraj bhai is a Carpenter. He wants to make a door and a table. He has a Metre rod only to measure length of wood needed. Can you tell which of the following will be more than 1 metre?
    A. Length of the door
    B. Length of the table
    C. Width of the table
    D. Width of the door

17. Length of a pencil can be measured in _____

    A. Yard   B. Miles
    C. Inches   D. None of these

18. Ricky uses his math book to do his homework. What tool can he use to measure the length of his math book?

    A. Ruler   B. Yardstick
    C. Hand   D. Feets

Direction (19-20) : Read the passage given below and answer the questions that follow:

Spiderman organized a long jump competition for the students of class 3. Many students took part in the competition. Everybody was very excited with it. After spiderman, Minku, Rinku, Tinku, Chinku, Pinku and Dinku jumped. Minku started the game by jumping at distance of 2 metres. Pinku's jump was 3 and half metre long. Then Tinki jumped at a distance of 250 centimeter while Chinku jumped at a distance of 300 centimeter. Dinku's jump was 3 metre long and Rinku's jump was 2 and half metre long. When the game ended spiderman recorded the distances jumped by children.

19. Who is the winner of the competition?
    A. Pinku   B. Tinku
    C. Chinku D. Rinku

20. Who jumped the least distance?
    A. Minku   B. Rinku
    C. Dinku   D. Tinku

Answer Key

1. C	2. D	3. B	4. D	5. A	6. B	7. A	8. D
9. B	10. A	11. B	12. C	13. D	14. A	15. B	16. A
17. C	18. A	19. A	20. A				

Hints and Solutions

3. Clearly measuring tape measures in meter.
4. Distance from house to school is in kilometers
5. Frock (4 m) requires maximum length of cloth.
6. Shorts requires minimum length of cloth
7. Statement A is incorrect
10. We know standard unit of length is meter.
11. Cloth merchant use a Meter rod to measure cloths.
14. 1 decimeter = 10 centimeters.
15. A 15-centimeter scale can measure length up to 15 cm.

17. Length of a pencil can be measured inches
    Distance covered by Minku = 2m
    Distance covered by Pinku = 3.5m
    Distance covered by Tinku = 2.50 m
    　　　　　　　　　　　　　 = 2.5 m
    Distance covered by Chinku = 300cm
    　　　　　　　　　　　　　　 = 3m
    Distance covered by Dinku = 3 m
    Distance covered by Rinku = 2.5 m
19. Hence winner of the competition
    　　　　　　　　　　　　　 = Pinku
20. Minku jumped the least distance.

Unit – 7 : Length

Unit - 8 : Weight

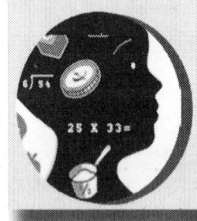

Learning Objectives : In this unit, we will learn about:
- Weight
- Measuring weight
- Conversion Factors

Weight

The weight of an item is the measure of its heaviness, that is how heavy the item is. Different items have different weights.

Check out the different types of weighing devices given below:

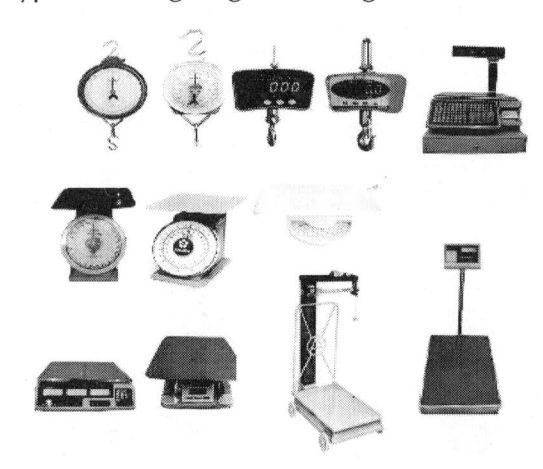

They all are weighing scale. These are used for different purposes.
  (i) To weigh small babies
  (ii) To weigh body weight
  (iii) To weigh things like vegetables, grains, etc.
  (iv) To weigh junk or various other things
  (v) At shops

Unit of Weight

We measure weight in terms of standard units of kilogram and grams. The standard unit of mass is kilogram. The mass of rice, sugar, vegetables and other commodities are weighed in terms of kilograms and grams.

Gram is the smallest unit of mass. kg is the short form of 'kilogram and (g) is the short form of gram. Here are some common weights used with weighing scales.

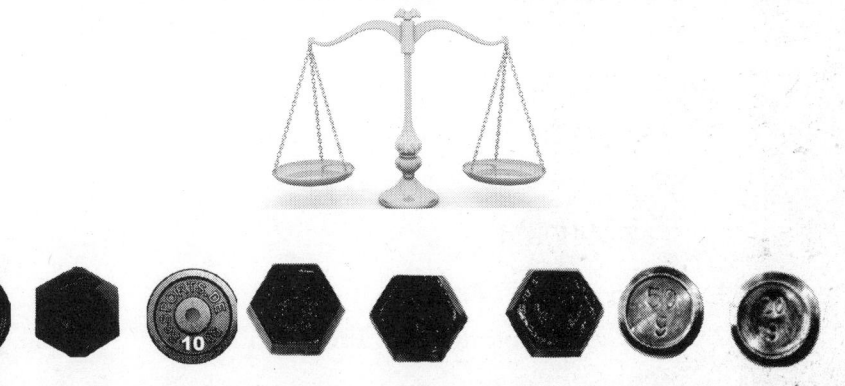

Alongwith these smaller weights like 1g, 2g, 5g, 10g and 20g are also used. These are used to weight very light things like ornaments etc.

Examples:
(A) A paperclip weighs about 1 gram.

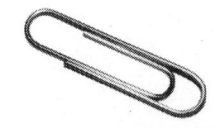

(B) We can weight our body using weighing machine.

Measuring Weight

1.	Look at the item carefully
2.	Choose a unit of weight
3.	Estimate the weight of the item in that unit
4.	Verify the weight using weighing balance

Note :
- The kilogram is the base unit of mass in the International System of Units.
- The kilogram is equal to mass of one liter of water.
- Always start from '0' while using weighing balance.

Conversion Factors
1 dekagram (dag) = 10 gram
1 hectogram (hg) = 10 dekagram
1 kilogram (kg) = 1000 gram
1 centigram (cg) = 10 milligram (mg)

Unit - 8 : Weight

1 decigram (dg) = 10 centigram (cg)
1 gram (gm) = 10 dg = 1000 mg

Misconcept / Concept

Misconcept : All the units of measuring the volume are equal.

Concept : Different units of measuring volume vary in the capacity. The volume must not be interchanged.

Misconcept : The object which looks bigger in size is heavier than the object which looks smaller in size.

Concept : The size of an object is not linked with its weight.

Misconcept : While using a weighing balance, the reading of the scale start from 1 since the counting of number starts term 1.

Concept : The reading of the scale on a weighing balance always starts from 0 not 1.

Multiple Choice Questions

1. Aana's mom wants to make a cake. She bought 486 gm of flour, 200 gm of eggs and 180 gm of sugar. What is the total weight of the ingredients that Aana bought?
   A. 864 gm B. 865 gm
   C. 866 gm D. 867 gm

2. Arushi had one kg of cherries. After she gave some to Neetu, she still has 380 gm left. How heavy were the cherries that Arushi gave to Neetu?
   A. 600 gm B. 610 gm
   C. 620 gm D. 630 gm

3. The limit of baggage that each person can bring in the Aeroplane is 22 kg. Golu's baggage weighs 26000 gm. How much over the limits is Golu's baggage?
   A. 3 kg B. 4 kg
   C. 5 kg D. 6 kg

4. Viru's mom bought 18 kg of rice, while Jaggi and Billu's mom bought 14 kg and 21 kg of rice respectively. What is total weight of rice that was bought?
   A. 50 kg B. 51 kg
   C. 52 kg D. 53 kg

5. A tube of Colgate toothpaste weighed 180 gm. Nitin's mother bought seven tubes. How many kilograms did the tubes of Colgate toothpaste weighed in total?
   A. 1 kg 240 gm B. 1 kg 250 gm
   C. 1 kg 260 gm D. 1 kg 270 gm

6. Rajesh is packing baskets of apples. Each apple weigh 17 gm. If there are 8 apples in each basket then how many grams of apple there are in each basket?
   A. 135 gm B. 136 gm
   C. 137 gm D. 138 gm

7. How many grams does one kilogram has?
   A. 10 gm B. 100 gm
   C. 1 gm D. 1000 gm

8. Sudhir was estimating weight of some objects and wrote few sentence. But one of them is wrong. Can you find the wrong statement?
   1. An electric iron is lighter than a chair.
   2. Perfume bottle is heavier than a comb.
   3. A watch is heavier than a hairband.
   4. A hairband is lighter than a rubber band.

   A. 2 B. 1
   C. 4 D. 3

9. Bunny was watching National Geographic channel and saw different animals. He started thinking about their weights and noted about them a paper. There were some mistakes in his estimate. Find the mistake and choose the correct option based on true or false.
   1. Weight of elephant is more than 1000 kg.
   2. Weight of a big snake is less than 10 kg.
   3. Weight of a fox is less than 50 kg.

Unit-8 : Weight

4. Weight of lion is more than 200 kg.
   A. TFTF   B. FTFT
   C. FTTF   D. TFFT

Direction (10-11) : Ashu wants to know the weight of some objects. He made a list of objects whose weight is less than 1kg and another list of objects whose weight is more than 1 kg. But he made a mistake in both the lists. Can you find the odd one in both the lists?

10. Objects the weight more than 1 kg
    A. A big water melon
    B. T.V.
    C. Shoes
    D. Table

11. Objects with weight less than 1 kg
    A. Pencil box
    B. Hand bag
    C. Water bottle
    D. An iron wardrobe

Direction (12-13) : Pragya was visiting a market. She saw all types of vegetables and fruits in various sizes. She wanted to know their weight, so she picked them one by one as given below. Order the vegetable given below from heaviest to lightest to help Pragya.

12.
   A. Pumpkin
   B. Brinjal
   C. Tomato
   D. Lady finger
   A. BACD   B. DCBA
   C. ABCD   D. ACBD

13.
   A. Pineapple   B. Cherry
   C. Mango   D. Chikoo
   A. ACDB   B. CADB
   C. CABD   D. ACBD

Direction (14-15) : Read the passage and answer the questions.

Kajal loves cats. She had four cats. One day she decided to note down their weights in order to keep a check on their health. She found that her eldest cat Lili weighs 2 kg more than Mili while Mili weighs 3 kg less than Kili. She had another cat Sili which was 1 kg lighter than Mili and was of 6 kgs?

14. Who is the heaviest cat?
    A. Lili   B. Mili
    C. Kili   D. Sili

15. Who is the lightest cat ?
    A. Lili   B. Mili
    C. Kili   D. Sili

Direction (16-17) : Tony Bua made a list of items she required for her kitchen. She prepared a table of items and their weights. Read the table below and answer the questions that below :

S. No.	Items	Weight
1	Wheat flour	More than 1 kg
2	Sugar	More than 1 kg
3	Butter	Less than 1 kg
4	Ghee	1kg
5	Curd	Less than 1 kg
6	Oil	1 kg

16. Sugar : Wheat Flour :: ? : Oil
    A. Butter   B. Ghee
    C. Curd   D. Sugar

17. Butter : Less than 1 kg :: ? : more than 1 kg.
    A. Oil   B. Ghee
    C. Wheat Flour   D. Curd

Directions (18-20) : Read the following table and answer the questions that follow:

Weight	Rate
0 – 5kg	₹ 20
6 –10 kg	₹ 40
11–20 kg	₹ 60
21–30 kg	₹ 80

18. Tripti weighted her pumpkin on the scale and found it was 7 kg. How much did her pumpkin cost?
    A. ₹ 20
    B. ₹ 40
    C. ₹ 60
    D. ₹ 80

19. Chotu weighted his pumpkin on the scale and found it was 12000 gm. How much did his pumpkin cost?
    A. ₹ 20
    B. ₹ 40
    C. ₹ 60
    D. ₹ 80

20. Prateek's pumpkin weighed 200 gm. How much did his pumpkin cost?
    A. ₹ 20
    B. ₹ 40
    C. ₹ 60
    D. ₹ 80

Answer Key

1. C	2. C	3. B	4. D	5. C	6. B	7. D	8. C
9. D	10. C	11. D	12. C	13. A	14. C	15. D	16. B
17. C	18. B	19. C	20. A				

Unit - 8 : Weight

Hints and Solutions

1. Total weight of the ingredients
 = (486 + 200 + 180) gm
2. Required weight = 1 kg – 380 gm
 = (1000 – 380) gm = 620 gm
4. Total weight of rice = 18 + 14 + 21
 = 53 kg
5. Required weight = 7 × 180 gm
 = 1260 gm = 1 kg 260 gm.
7. 1 kg = 1000 gm
8. Statement C is incorrect.
10. Shoes's weight is less than 1 kg.
12. The correct order is ABCD.

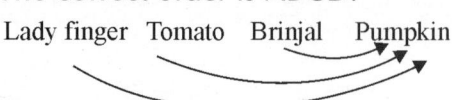

 Lady finger   Tomato   Brinjal   Pumpkin

13. The correct order is ACDB.
18. Tripti weighted her pumpkin on the scale and found it was 7 kg. Hence pumpkin's cost is ₹ 40.
19. Pumpkin's cost = 12000 gm = 12 kg
 ∴ Rate is ₹ 60.
20. Prateek's pumpkin weight = 200 gm
 ∴ Rate is ₹ 20.

Unit-9 : Capacity

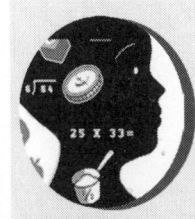

Learning Objectives : In this unit, we will learn about:
- Capacity
- Volume
- Measuring Capacity

Capacity

The capacity of a container is the amount of liquid it can hold. The vessels which are larger in size can hold more liquid as compared to the vessels which are smaller in size. The standard unit for measuring the capacity of a container is litre.

$$1 \text{ liter} = 1000 \text{ milliliters}$$

Example : The bucket has a capacity of 9 liters.

Liquids are measured by special vessels. Some of the common types of such vessels are shown below.

1 Liter   **500 ml**   **200 ml**

Volume

It is the amount of space occupied by an item. Units of volume can be liters and milliliters for liquids. For solids cubic centimeters or cubic meters are used as a units of volume.

Items that may require liters to measure them are :
- A carton of ice-cream.
- Amount of water consumed in a day by a human being, e.g. Shraddha drinks 5 liters of water a day.
- Items that may require milliliters to measure them are :
  (i) A glass of water

Unit-9 : Capacity   61

(ii) A bottle of perfume. Example : Shraddha's perfume bottle weighs 50 ml.

Measuring Capacity
- Take a container whose capacity is to be determined.

- Take a water bottle whose capacity is 1 litre.

- Fill the water bottle completely
- Pour the water into the container whose capacity is to be measured.
- Count the number of times you filled the container using water bottle.

Shortcut to problem solving
To accurately measure the quantity of something jars with measuring scales should be used. A measuring jar contains pre-defined scales marked on the glass or plastic jar and given the exact volume measure.

Volume conversion factors
$$1 \text{ liter (l)} = 10 \text{ deciliter (dl)}$$
$$1 \text{ centiliter (cl)} = 10 \text{ milliliter (ml)}$$
$$1 \text{ liter (l)} = 1000 \text{ milliliter (ml)}$$
$$1 \text{ deciliter (dl)} = 10 \text{ centiliter (cl)}$$

Misconcept / Concept
Misconcept : Capacity of a container is same as volume of the liquid in it.

Concept : There is a confusion between liquid volume and capacity of container. The capacity of container is not always same as volume of the liquid in it. For example, a milk bottle have the capacity of 250ml of milk but the volume of milk in it could be100ml only.

Misconcept : The volume of the liquid gets changed when it is poured from one container to another container of a different size. There is more liquid in the one that has the highest level.

Concept : The volume of the liquid does not change when the same is poured from one container to another container of a different size. It only takes the shape of the container.

Multiple Choice Questions

Direction (1-3) : Shraddha wants to fill a kettle (1 lt), bowl (750 ml), bottle (500 ml) with water. She has a glass (250 ml) with him. Can you estimate the number of glasses of water she needs to fill?

1. In a Kettle
   A. 2   B. 3
   C. 4   D. 5

2. In a Bowl
   A. 2   B. 3
   C. 4   D. 5

3. In a Bottle
   A. 2   B. 3
   C. 4   D. 5

4. A big tank has a capacity of 900 liters. If there is already 450 liters in the tank, how more water is needed to fill up completely?
   A. 500   B. 450
   C. 350   D. 400

5. Aryaveer drank twenty liter of water. Golu drank 3liters of water less than Aryaveer. How much water did they drink altogether?
   A. 16   B. 15
   C. 37   D. 18

6. If we convert 5 liter into milliliter, we will get?
   A. 5000 ml   B. 50 ml
   C. 500 ml   D. None of these

7. Convert 4723ml into liters and milliliters.
   A. 4 l 723 ml   B. 47 l 23 ml
   C. 4 ml 723 l   D. 47 ml 23 l

8. A shop has a sale of 40 liter of juice every day. The neighboring juice shop sells five times as much. How much does the neighboring shop sells?
   A. 150 lt   B. 200 lt
   C. 250 lt   D. 300 lt

9. Pradeep drinks five 200 ml glasses of milk every day. How many liter of milk he drink each day?
   A. 5 liters   B. 3 liters
   C. 2 liters   D. 1 liters

10. Maya opened a bottle containing 1 liter of juice. If she shared the juice equally with her uncle Arun. How many milliliters of juice will each of them get?
    A. 20 ml   B. 50 ml
    C. 200 ml   D. 500 ml

11. If you want to fill your swimming pool up with then, which container would you use?
    A. Glass   B. Mug
    C. Bucket   D. Pan

12. If students of class 3 are going for a big picnic then which lemonade should be bought?
    A. Can   B. 5 liter bottle
    C. 1 liter bottle   D. Small carton

13. If 2540 ml : 2 lt 540 ml :: ? : : 1 lt 5 ml
    A. 1050 ml   B. 1500 ml
    C. 5001 ml   D. 1005 ml

14. If 3 lt 69 ml : 3069 ml :: ? : 3020 ml
    A. 3 l 20 ml   B. 3 l 200 ml
    C. 3 l 2 ml   D. 3 lt 2000 ml

Unit-9 : Capacity

15. How many buckets of water are needed to fill the water cooler of capacity 45 l? When the capacity of bucket is 5lts.
    A. 6
    B. 7
    C. 8
    D. 9

16. My aunty collected all different container and started thinking about their capacities. She wrote few sentences about them. Write true /false for the sentences she wrote.
    A: A cup can hold more coffee than a saucepan.
    B: A spoon can hold less sugar than a bowl.
    C: A glass can hold more water than a bottle.
    D : A saucepan can hold more tea than a cup.
    A. FFFT
    B. TFFT
    C. FTFT
    D. FFFF

17. A chef had 1lt of oil. After using the oil for the recipies he was left with 175 ml of oil. How much did he use for the recipies?
    A. 625 ml
    B. 725 ml
    C. 825 ml
    D. 925 ml

18. How many mugs (500 ml) of water are needed to fill a bucket (4 l)?
    A. 5
    B. 6
    C. 7
    D. 8

19. How many glasses (200ml) of milk are needed to fill 1lt jug?
    A. 5
    B. 6
    C. 7
    D. 8

20. How many cups (10ml) of oil are needed to fill a 2lt frying pan?
    A. 5
    B. 6
    C. 7
    D. 8

Answer Key

1. C	2. B	3. A	4. B	5. C	6. A	7. A	8. B
9. D	10. D	11. C	12. B	13. D	14. A	15. D	16. C
17. C	18. D	19. A	20. C				

Hints and Solutions

1. The numbers of glasses of water Shraddha needs to fill in a kettle $= \dfrac{1000}{250} = 4$

2. The numbers of glasses of water Shraddha needs to fill in a bowl $= \dfrac{750}{250} = 3$

3. The numbers of glasses of water Shraddha to fill in a Bottle $= \dfrac{500}{250} = 2$

4. Required amount of water $= 900 - 450$
   $= 450$ liters

6. $\because$ 1 Liter $= 1000$ ml
   $\therefore$ 5 Liters $= 5 \times 1000 = 5000$ ml

10. Maya and her uncle get $= \dfrac{1000}{2}$
    $= 500$ ml juice

13. $\because$ 2540 ml $= 2000$ ml $+ 540$ ml
    $= 2$ lt $+ 540$ ml
    $= 2$ lt, 540 ml
    $\therefore$ 1 lt 5 ml $= (1000 + 5)$ ml
    $= 1005$ ml

15. Capacity of bucket $= \dfrac{45}{5} = 9$ l

18. Here capacity of bucket $= 4$ l
    and capacity of my $= 500$ ml
    $\therefore$ No of mugs needed to fill a bucket
    $= \dfrac{4000}{500} = 8$

Unit – 9 : Capacity

Unit - 10 : Time

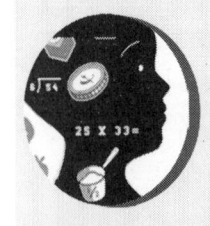

Learning Objectives : In this unit, we will learn about:
- Time
- Calendar

Time

A clock has three hands, a second hand, minute hand and an hour hand. These are fine small division between two successive numbers. So these are 60 small divisions in all. Each big division represents an hour. A clock helps us in knowing time and each small division represents a minute.
- The thinnest hand which is moving very fast is the second hand.
- The longest hand is minute hand.
- The shortest hand is hour hand.

Reading Time

In order to read the clock, look at the hour hand first and then look at the minute hand. For example, if the hour hand is at '4' and minute hand is at '12' then the time is 4 O'clock.

If the minute hand is at
- '1' it means 5 minutes have past so the time will become 4:05.
- '2' it means 10 minutes have past so the time will become 4:10.
- '3' it means 15 minutes have past so the time will become 4:15.
- '4' it means 20 minutes have past so the time will become 4:20.
- '5' it means 25 minutes have past so the time will become 4:25.
- '6' it means 30 minutes have past so the time will become 4:30.
- '7' it means 35 minutes have past so the time will become 4:35.

- '8' it means 40 minutes have past so the time will become 4:40.
- '9' it means 45 minutes have past so the time will become 4:45
- '10' it means 50 minutes have past so the time will become 4:50
- '11' it means 55 minutes have past so the time will become 4:55

Then again the minute hand has comes at '12', now the hour hand will come at '5' so the time will become 5 O' clock.

Time as a Fraction

Half (1/2) of an hour $\frac{60}{2}$ = 30 minutes

($\because$ 1 hour = 60 minutes)

and one fourth (1/4) of an hour = $\frac{60}{4}$ = 15 minutes

and one fourth (1/4) of an hour $\frac{60}{4}$ = 15 minutes

Look at the clock on the right

In the given clock, the hour hand is between 10 and 11, The minute hand is at 6. The time is 1/2 hour past 10 or half past ten. It is written as 10:30.

The time between one midnight and the next midnight is called one day. The hour hand goes twice round the clock face in one day. In one round the hour hand completes

Unit – 10 : Time

12 hour and hence in two rounds it completes 24 hours.
Hence, 1 day = 24 hours.

In the adjoining clock, the hour hand is at 6. The minute hand is at 3. The time is 1/4 hour after 6 or quarter part six. It is written as 6:15.

In the below clock the hour hand is between 5 and 6. The minute hand is at 9. The time is 1/4 hour before 6 or quarter to six. It is written as 5: 45.

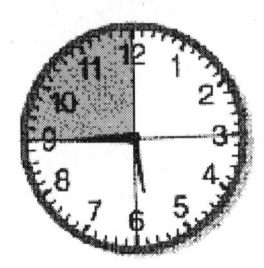

Calendar

A year has 12 months called calendar months. January is the first month of the year and December is the last month of the year.

The months of the year with the numbers of days in each are given below:

January	31	February	28 or 29
March	31	April	30
May	31	June	30
July	31	August	31
September	30	October	31
November	30	December	31

Note : If the name of the month is not mentioned, month = 30 days

Leap year

There are 365 days in a year. A leap year has 366 days. An year which is exactly divisible by 4 is a leap year. e.g. 2000, 2004, 2008 etc. are leap years. February in a leap year is of 29 days.

A calendar helps us to know about days, weeks, months and years.

\multicolumn{7}{c	}{2014 JUNE}
SUNDAY	MONDAY	TUESDAY	WEDNESDAY	THURSDAY	FRIDAY	SATURDAY
1	2	3	4	5	6	7
8	9	10	11	12	13	14
15	16	17	18	19	20	21
22	23	24	25	26	27	28
29	30					

We read the calendar to tell the days and dates. For example, from above calendar 15th June falls on Sunday.

A date is written as follows :

Date/month/year example : 15/06/2014

Or

Date-month-year example : 15-11-2104

Or

Date month' year example : 15th June, 2014

Do you remember the date when you wished "Happy New Year" to your friend?

1st January 2014.

Do you remember the date when India got Independence?

15th August' 1947

Examples

Time : People cannot carry a clock with them so they wear a watch to keep a track of time

- At what time do you brush your teeth?
  6 O'clock
- At what time do you take bath?
  6:30
- At what time does your family have dinner?
  9 O' clock
- Do you check the time when you go to bed?
  11:30

Unit – 10 : Time

Multiple Choice Questions

1. If brushing : minutes, then sleeping : ?
   A. Seconds
   B. Hours
   C. Days
   D. Months

2. Find the odd one out.
   A. 10/ 11/ 2001
   B. 5/ 17/ 2001
   C. 17/ 5/ 2001
   D. 11/ 10/ 2001

3. AM refers to which part of the day?
   A. Morning
   B. Afternoon
   C. Evening
   D. Night

4. The sun is at its peek at what time of the day?
   A. Morning
   B. Noon
   C. Evening
   D. Night

5. Moon shines bright during which time of the day?
   A. Morning
   B. Noon
   C. Evening
   D. Night

6. Noon time refers to :
   A. 12 pm
   B. 12 am
   C. 11:55 pm
   D. 11:55 am

7. What is the difference between 9:30 am and 11:00am?
   A. 1 hour
   B. 1 hour 15minutes
   C. 1hour 30minutes
   D. 2hours

8. What is the ideal lunch time?
   A. 2:00 pm
   B. 5:00 pm
   C. 8:00 am
   D. 8:00 pm

9. What time is referred as midnight?
   A. 12am
   B. 12 pm
   C. 1pm
   D. 2 am

10. Which month of the year has the least number of days?
    A. January
    B. July
    C. May
    D. February

11. Which of the following represents the time 5minute past 8?
    A. 7:55
    B. 8:55
    C. 8:05
    D. 8:20

12. In the 24 hour format, what time is actually represented as 17:30?
    A. 4:30 pm
    B. 5:30 pm
    C. 3:30 pm
    D. 6:30 pm

13. Anil practices piano daily 15minutes. How many minutes does he practice in 4 days?
    A. 1hour
    B. 50 minutes
    C. 1hour 15minutes
    D. 2hours

14. If 12/03/2014 : 12th March'2014' then 06/07/2013: ?
    A. 7th June' 2013
    B. 6th June' 2013
    C. 6th July'2013
    D. 7th July'2013

Direction (15-16) : Based on the given calendar, answer the following questions :

June 2014

Sunday	Monday	Tuesday	Wednesday	Thursday	Friday	Saturday
1	2	3	4	5	6	7
8	9	10	11	12	13	14
15	16	17	18	19	20	21
22	23	24	25	26	27	28
29	30					

15. What day of the week is June 22?
    A. Sunday   B. Monday
    C. Thursday   D. Saturday

16. What date is the third Sunday in June?
    A. 7   B. 28
    C. 15   D. 21

Direction (17-20) : Use numbers (0-9) only to answer the questions given below:

17. How many days are there between Monday and Thursday?
    A. 1   B. 2
    C. 3   D. 4

18. How many weeks are there in a month?
    A. 1   B. 2
    C. 3   D. 4

19. How many minutes are passed if the 'minute' hand is at 1?
    A. 5   B. 4
    C. 3   D. 2

20. How many minutes will it take from 3:10 to 3:17?
    A. 6   B. 5
    C. 8   D. 7

Answer Key

1. B	2. B	3. A	4. B	5. D	6. A	7. C	8. A
9. A	10. D	11. C	12. B	13. A	14. C	15. A	16. C
17. B	18. D	19. A	20. D				

Hints and Solutions

12. In the 24 hour format
    17 : 30 = 12 + 5 : 30 = 5 : 30 pm.

13. Anil practices piano in 4 days
    = 4 × 15 = 60 minutes = 1 hour

15. June 22 in on Sunday.

16. Third Sunday in June is on 15.

20. Required time = 3 : 17 − 3 : 10
    = 7 minutes.

Unit – 10 : Time

Unit - 11 : Money

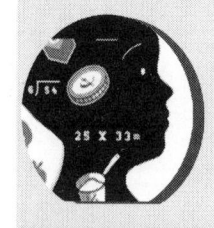

Learning Objectives : In this unit, we will learn about:
- Money
- Important Facts about Money

Money

Money is primarily a medium of exchange. It is a way for a person to trade what he has for what he wants.

Money is generally accepted as payment for goods and services. Money is also known as Currency.

Main functions of money are
 (i) Medium of exchange
 (ii) Store of value
 (iii) A unit of account

Hence any item that fulfils these functions can be considered money.

Important Facts about Money

- In India the unit of money is rupees. It is denoted by the symbol ' ₹ '.
  1 Rupee = 100 paisa.
- Other important currencies in the world are USD $ (United States Dollar which is used in America), GBP (UK Pound Sterling £) used in United Kingdom and Euro used in Europe.
- Money in India comes in form of paper as well as coins.
  In short, we write ₹ for rupee, P for paisa
  10 coins of 10 paisa make one Rupee.
  2 coins of 50 paisa make one Rupee.
  4 coins of 25 paisa make one Rupee.
  1 coin of 50 paisa and 2 cons of 25 paisa make one Rupee.
- The paper based notes available in India are of ₹ 1000, ₹ 500, ₹ 100, ₹ 50, ₹ 20, ₹ 5 as shown below :

- Till few year back there were paper notes for ₹ 2 and ₹ 1 as well but they are no longer in use but are still valid. Their picture is as shown below:

- The coins available in India are of ₹ 10, ₹ 5, ₹ 2 and ₹ 1 as shown below:

Unit–11 : Money

Did You Know?
- Paper notes are called bank notes as they are issued by the Reserve Bank of India (RBI).
- Picture of Mahatma Gandhi, father of the nation, is printed on every note.
- Every note contains signature of RBI Governor.
- As the value of currency increases, the size of the paper note also increases.

Misconcept /Concept
Misconcept : If a paper note is mutilated or torn, then you feel that it cannot be used as no shopkeeper is ready to take it.

Concept : Torn or spoilt notes can be exchanged in banks and they will give you Money depending on the condition of the note.

Multiple Choice Questions

Direction (1-4) : Fill in the blanks in question 1 to 4 to get the resultant money.

1. ₹ 20 + ₹ 40 + _____ = ₹ 160
   A. ₹ 50
   B. ₹ 100
   C. ₹ 70
   D. ₹ 60

2. ₹ 30 + ₹ 80 + ₹ 25 + ------- = ₹ 150, 50p
   A. ₹ 50,50p
   B. ₹ 25,50p
   C. ₹ 20.25p
   D. ₹ 15,50p

3. ₹ 15 + ₹ 25 + ------ = ₹ 100
   A. ₹ 60
   B. ₹ 70
   C. ₹ 80
   D. ₹ 50

4. ₹ 75 + ₹ 20 + ------ = ₹ 150
   A. ₹ 45
   B. ₹ 50
   C. ₹ 55
   D. ₹ 70

Direction (5-9) : Consider the price of these items below to answer the questions.

₹ 4.50 per banana
₹ 170 for one clock
₹ 2.75 per pencil
₹ 7.50 per chocolate

5. The cost of one dozen bananas will be ----------.
   A. ₹ 45
   B. ₹ 48
   C. ₹ 54
   D. ₹ 52

6. If Ajay wants to buy one pencil and two chocolates, how much he needs to pay?
   A. ₹ 15
   B. ₹ 16.50
   C. ₹ 17
   D. ₹ 17.75

7. Four chocolates can be bought for ₹ 30 and two pencils can be bought for ₹ 5. This statement is ------- .
   A. True
   B. False
   C. Insufficient information
   D. None of these

8. If he has a five hundred rupees note. He wants to buy as many clocks he can with this amount. How many clocks can he buy?
   A. 1
   B. 2
   C. 3
   D. 4

9. Which of the following statement is not true?
   A. Cost of (2 banana + 1 pencil) > Cost of 1 chocolate
   B. Cost of (1 banana + 1 pencil) < Cost of 1 chocolate
   C. Cost of (1 banana + 2 pencils) > Cost of 1 chocolate
   D. Cost of (2 bananas + 2 pencils) > Cost of 2 chocolates

10. Identify the total value of the combination of money.
    ₹ 5, ₹ 10, ₹ 20, ₹ 50, ₹ 500, 50 p, 25 p
    A. ₹ 600, 25 p
    B. ₹ 550, 75 p
    C. ₹ 480, 50 p
    D. ₹ 585, 75 p

11. Calculate the total value of the combination of money.
    ₹ 10, ₹ 10, ₹ 5, ₹ 1, ₹ 2, ₹ 50, ₹ 100
    A. ₹ 175
    B. ₹ 80
    C. ₹ 178
    D. ₹ 115

12. Raju earned ₹ 5 everyday during September. How much money did he earn in the whole month?
    A. ₹ 200
    B. ₹ 180
    C. ₹ 150
    D. ₹ 70

Unit – 11 : Money

13. In May, Ankita earned ₹ 10 everyday for helping her mother in doing house hold chores she spent ₹ 95. How much she is left with?
    A. ₹ 215
    B. ₹ 180
    C. ₹ 200
    D. ₹ 310

14. Monu want to purchase books and gave following money to cashier. Four coins of ₹ 2, two notes of ₹ 20, three notes of ₹ 100. If the price of books were ₹ 326, how much change will he get back?
    A. ₹ 20
    B. ₹ 22
    C. ₹ 25
    D. ₹ 28

15. Shraddha bought 6 chocolates. All the chocolates were of the same price. The total cost was ₹ 88.50. How much money did each chocolate cost?
    A. 14 rupees
    B. 14 rupees and 05 paisa
    C. 14 rupees and 50 paisa
    D. 14 rupees and 75 paisa

16. If Shubhra bought oranges for ₹ 75 and she paid ₹ 100 to fruit seller, which expression shows the correct amount of change that she will get back?
    A. 100 + 75
    B. 100 − 75
    C. 100/75
    D. 100 × 75

17. Arrange the following amounts of money in ascending order:
    ₹ 2.75 ₹ 1.75 ₹ 2.25 ₹ 2.50 ₹ 1.50 ₹ 0.75
    A. ₹ 0.75 < ₹ 1.50 < ₹ 1.75 < ₹ 2.50 < ₹2.25 < ₹ 2.75
    B. ₹ 1.75 < ₹ 1.50 < ₹ 0.75 < ₹ 2.25 < ₹ 2.50 < ₹ 2.75
    C. ₹ 0.75 < ₹ 1.50 < ₹ 1.75 < ₹ 2.25 < ₹ 2.50 < ₹ 2.75
    D. ₹ 0.75 < ₹ 1.75 < ₹ 1.50 < ₹ 2.25 < ₹ 2.50 < ₹ 2.75

18. Arrange the following amounts of money in descending order :
    ₹ 10.75 , ₹ 10.65 , ₹ 11.25, ₹ 11.05 ₹ 12.50, ₹ 10.55
    A. ₹ 12.50 > ₹ 11.25 > ₹ 11.05 > ₹ 10.75 > ₹ 10.65 > ₹ 10.55
    B. ₹ 12.50 > ₹ 11.05 > ₹ 11.25 > ₹ 10.75 > ₹ 10.65 > ₹ 10.55
    C. ₹ 12.50 > ₹ 11.25 > ₹ 11.05 > ₹ 10.55 > ₹ 10.65 > ₹ 10.75
    D. ₹ 12.50 > ₹ 11.25 > ₹ 11.05 > ₹ 10.65 > ₹ 10.75 > ₹ 10.55

Direction (19-21) : Consider the following scenario to answer the questions :

Navneet went to watch a cricket match in the stadium. He had ₹ 800 with him. He paid ₹ 200 for the ticket and a cap for ₹ 50. Inside the stadium he bought a cold drink for ₹ 20. At the end of the match he donated ₹ 50 to the charity club maintained by stadium officials.

19. How much money is left with Navneet now?
    A. ₹ 480
    B. ₹ 320
    C. ₹ 580
    D. ₹ 450

20. The total amount spend by Navneet is _____.
    A. ₹ 320
    B. ₹ 340
    C. ₹ 270
    D. ₹ 120

21. On the way back to home, Navneet saw a book store. He bought a book for ₹ 100. Now, how much money is left with him?

A. ₹ 480   B. ₹ 380
C. ₹ 100   D. ₹ 420

Direction (22-25): Consider the following story to answer the question.

Raj and his family (his father, mother and sister) went to summer vacation by a plane to an island. Age of Raj is 5 years and his sister is 1 year old. If the fare of flight is as follows:

For two adults one side fare : ₹ 5000

For 5-15 years old, one side fare : ₹ 2000

For less than 5 years old, one side fare : ₹ 500

They stayed in hotel for 4 days for which one day stays was ₹ 1000. Next morning they went for shopping in which his mother spent ₹ 5000 for clothing, his father spend ₹ 2000 to purchase a watch. Raj spent ₹ 100 on cookies. On second day, Raj and his father went for surfing for which charges were ₹ 1000 per person.

22. How much total money they spend on flight fare both the sides?
A. ₹ 12500   B. ₹ 15000
C. ₹ 30000   D. ₹ 5000

23. Find the amount spend for stay in the Hotel alone.
A. ₹ 1000   B. ₹ 2000
C. ₹ 3000   D. ₹ 4000

24. What is the total amount they spend on Raj's sister?
A. ₹ 500   B. ₹ 1000
C. ₹ 2000   D. ₹ 3000

25. The total amount spend on shopping is _____ .
A. ₹ 7100   B. ₹ 7200
C. ₹ 7000   D. None of thes

Answer Key

1. B	2. D	3. A	4. C	5. C	6. D	7. B	8. B
9. C	10. D	11. C	12. C	13. A	14. B	15. D	16. B
17. C	18. A	19. A	20. A	21. B	22. B	23. D	24. B
25. A							

Unit-11 : Money

Hints and Solutions

1. Resultant money = ₹ 20 + ₹ 40 + ?
   = ₹ 160
   ⇒ ? = 160 − 60 = ₹ 100
2. Here ₹ 30 + ₹ 80 + ₹ 25 + ? = ₹ 150.50
   ⇒ 135 + ? = 150.50
   ⇒ ? = 150.50 − 135 = 15.50 = ₹ 15.50 p
3. ? = ₹ 100 − ₹ (15 + 25) = ₹ 60
4. ? = ₹ 150 − ₹ 95 = ₹ 55
5. Total cost of one dozen banana
   = 12 × ₹ 4.50 = ₹ 54
   = cost of 1 pencil + cost of 2 chocolates
6. Total Money = ₹ 2.75 + 2 × 7.50
   = 2.75 + 15.00 = ₹ 17.75
7. Cost of 4 chocolates
   = 4 × cost of 1 chocolate
   = 4 × 7.50 = ₹ 30
   and cost of 2 pencils = 2 × 5.50
   Hence, false.
8. Required No. of clocks = $\frac{500}{170}$
   = 2 (₹ 160)
10. Total money
    = ₹ (5 + 10 + 20 + 50 + 500 + 0.50 + 0.25)
    = ₹ 585.75
12. There are 30 days in September
    Required amount = 5 × 30 = ₹ 150
14. Required amount
    = ₹ (3 × 100 + 20 × 2 + 4 × 2)
    = − ₹ 326
    = ₹ [(300 + 40 + 8) − 326] = ₹ 22
15. Cost of 1 chocolate = $\frac{88.50}{6}$ = 14.75
    = ₹ 14 and 75 paisa
17. The correct order is ₹ 2.75, ₹ 2.50, ₹ 2.25, ₹ 1.75, ₹ 1.50, ₹ 0.75
19. Required Money
    = 800 − (200 + 50 + 20 + 50)
    = 800 − 320 = ₹ 480
20. Clearly total amount spend by Raj is ₹ 320.
21. After buying book for ₹ 100. Required amount = 480 − 100 = 380

Unit-12 : Geometrical Shapes

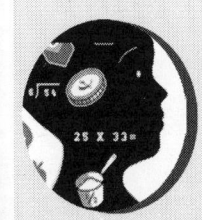

Learning Objectives : In this unit, we will learn about:
- Plane Figures
- Point
- Line
- Ray
- Congruent Figures
- Similar Figures

Plane Figures

Rectangle, square, triangle and circle are some of the common plane figures

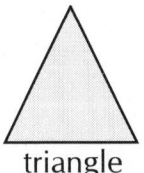

triangle
A polygon with 3 sides

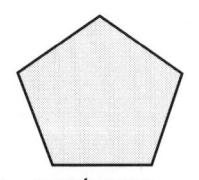

pentagon
A polygon with 5 sides

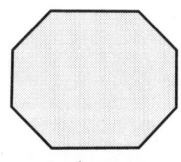

octagon
A polygon with 8 sides

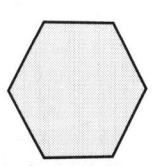

hexagon
A polygon with 6 sides

A 4-sided figure with 4 right angles and opposite sides parallel and the same length

A 4-sided figure that has 4 equal sides and 4 right angles

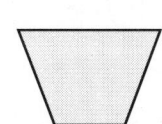

A 4-sided figure that has exactly one pair of parallel sides

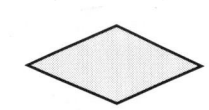

A 4-sided figure with 2 pairs of parallel sides and all sides the same length

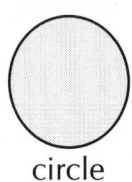

circle

Circle : A circle is a plane figure in which all the points are the same distance from a point called the center. A circle has no side and no vertex.

Solid Shapes : Cube, cuboid, sphere, cylinder and cone are solid shapes.

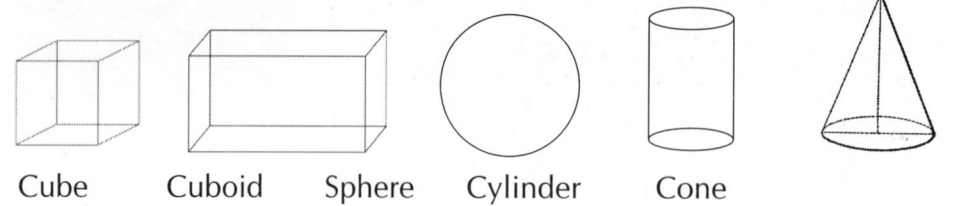

Cube   Cuboid   Sphere   Cylinder   Cone

We can use geometric shapes to help describe real-world objects.

Point

A point is the smallest geometrical shape. It does not have a length, breadth or thickness. The vertices of a rectangle, square or triangle are called points. To make a point we put a dot (.) on paper. We can name the points using capital letters A, B, C etc.

•
P

Line

The shortest distance between two points is called line. On joining any two points with a ruler and extending on both sides endlessly we get a line.

←——•————•——→
    A   B

A line neither has any end point nor a definite length.

Line Segment

On joining two points with a ruler we get a line segment. It has a beginning an ending point.

←————→
A   B

Ray

On joining two points with a ruler and extending endlessly on one side only, we get a ray

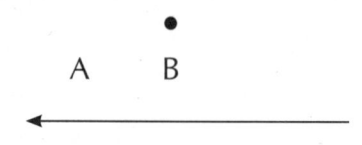

•
A B

←————————

Example : Identify the shape

The flag is a rectangle. It is a 4-sided figure with 4 right angles and opposite sides parallel and the same length.

Example : Name the shape

This sign is a triangle. It is a polygon with 3 sides.

Example : Identify the shape of the sign the boy is holding.

The sign the boy is holding is an octagon. It is a polygon with 8 sides

Summary of the properties of plane figures

	Properties	Rectangle	Square	Triangle
1.	No. of sides	4	4	3
2.	No. of corners	4	4	3
3.	No. of diagonals	2	2	0
4.	Are all the sides equal	no	yes	may or may not be
5.	Are the diagonals equal	yes	yes	x
6.	Are only the opposite sides equal	yes	No	may or may not be

Congruent Figures

Congruent figures are the same size and shape. These 2 rectangles are Congruent. They are the exact same size and shape.

Unit – 12 : Geometrical Shapes

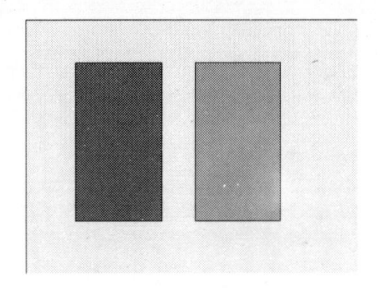

These 2 triangles are Congruent. They are the exact same size and shape.

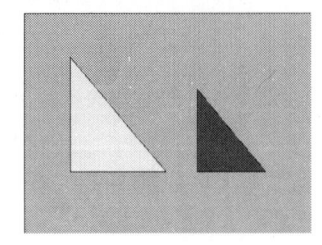

These 2 circles are **Congruent.** They are the exact same size and shape.

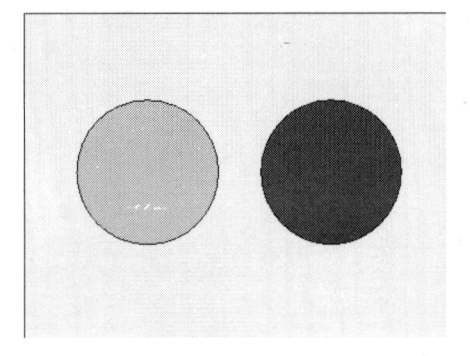

Similar Figures
Similar figures have the same shape, but are not the same size. These 2 rectangles are **Similar**. They are the same shape, but not the same size.

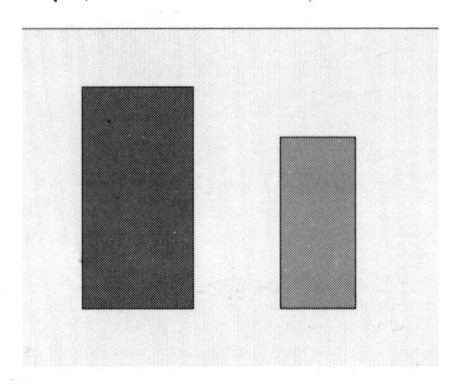

These two circles are similar. They are the same shape, but not the same size.

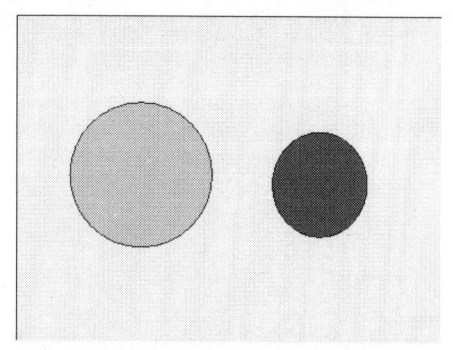

These two triangles are Similar. They are the same shape, but not the same size.

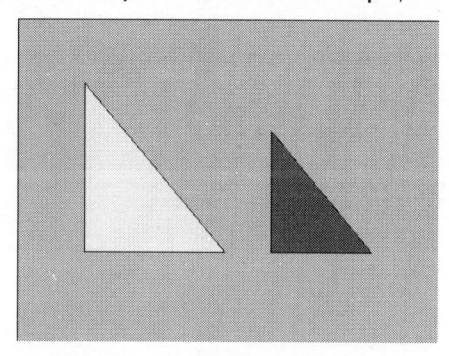

Similar figures are the same shape, but not the same size.

Straight Line
If we stretch a thread tightly, we get a straight line. Squares, rectangles and triangles are made of straight lines.

straight line

Curved Line
If we hold the thread loosely, we get a curved line. Circles and Ovals are made of curved lines.

curved line

Straight Lines and Curved Lines
Straight line is the smallest distance between two points which is not curved in any direction and continuous in the same direction. It can be horizontal, vertical of slanting.

Slanting line
It is also defined as a line with zero curvature. It minimizes the distance between the two points.

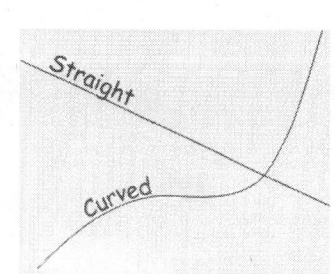

Unit - 12 : Geometrical Shapes

The above figure shows that the straight line is a line that does not have curve. The straight line is uniquely defined by the twos points. For example, if the line is defined by the two points A and B, then the straight line is defined as $\overline{AB}$.

Equation of a Straight Line
A straight line is defined by a linear equation whose general form is,
$$Ax + By + C = 0,$$
where, A, B are not equal to zero. and c is a constant.

Slope of a Straight Line
The equation of line with a given slope value m and the y-intercept b is $y = mx + b$, where b is constant.

Straight Line Construction
If a straight line meets another straight line, the adjacent angles so formed are supplementary. This is also called angles on one side of a Straight Line Theorem.

Proof for straight line theorem
A straight line CO meets straight line AB at O.
To Prove :
$$\angle AOC + \angle BOC = 180°$$

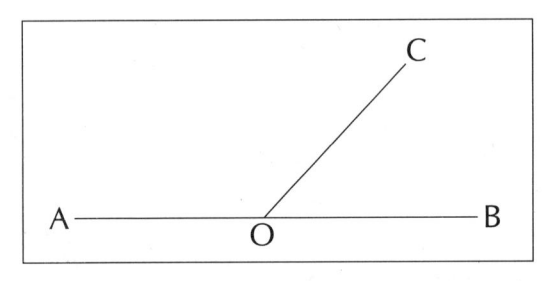

1. $\angle AOC + \angle BOC = \angle AOB$ (Since $\angle AOD$ is a straight line)
2. $\angle AOB = 180°$ (Straight Line)
3. Therefore, $\angle AOC + \angle BOC = 180°$ (From 1 and 2).

Straight Line Graph
For drawing the straight line we need to do the following steps.
1. Mark the first end point.
2. Mark the second end point.
3. Connect the two end points.

This is called as straight line.

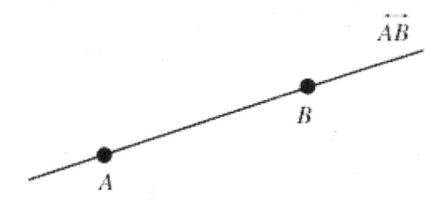

So, this is the straight line connecting the points A and B.

Distance between two Straight Lines

Let us find the distance between two points A and B having coordinates (x_1, y_1) and (x_2, y_2) respectively. Distance of straight line can be denoted as AB.

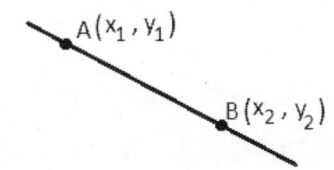

Straight line distance between two points is expressed as :

$$AB = \sqrt{(x_2 - x_1)^2 + (y_2 - y_2)^2}$$

Straight Line Examples

- The straight line at right angles to the another line is called as the perpendicular.
- The straight line that is limiting the value of the curve is called as asymptote.
- The straight line that just touches a curve or curved surface at a particular point but does not intersect it at that point is called as the tangent.
- The straight line that intersects the curve at two or the more points is called as the secant.
- The straight line from the center to the perimeter of the circle is called as the radius.
- The straight line connecting two points on a curve is called as the chord.
- The straight line relating any two vertices of the polygon that are not adjacent is called as the diagonal.

Given below are some straight line examples.

Example : Draw a Straight Line that connects the points(0, 5) and (6, 0).
Solution :
1. Mark the given points in a graph.
2. Connect the two end points

So, the Straight line connecting the above two points looks as follows :

Unit – 12 : Geometrical Shapes

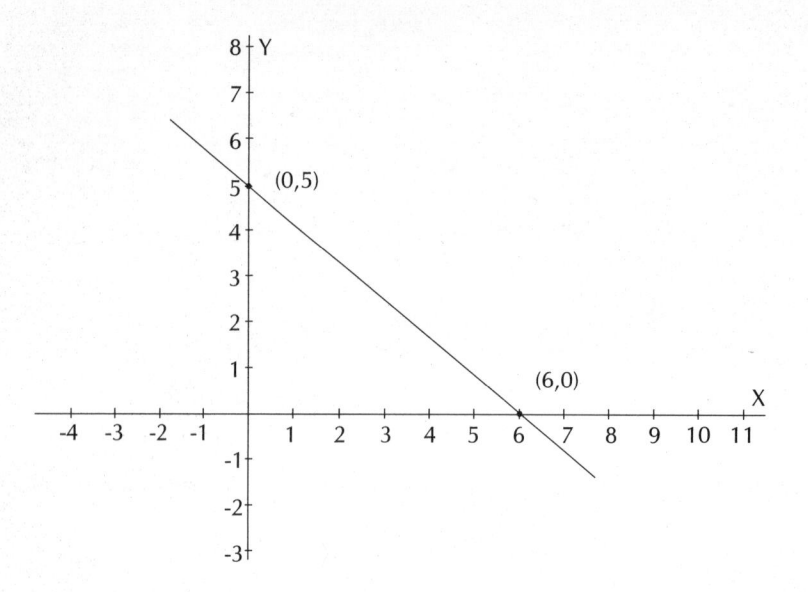

Example : Find the equation of the line passing through the intersection of the lines $6x + 5y = 11$, $8x - 5y = 3$ and parallel to the line $3x - 2y + 12 = 0$.

Solution : The given lines are

$$6x + 5y = 11 \qquad ...(i)$$
$$8x - 5y = 3 \qquad ...(ii)$$

Solving for x and y, the coordinates of the point of intersection of the two lines are (1, 1). The slope of the line through (1, 1) = Slope of line $3x - 2y + 12 = 0$. The equation of the line which passes through (1, 1) and whose slope is 32 is $(y - 1) = 32 (x - 1)$.

Example : The part of line intercepted between the axes is divided by the point (−5, 2) in the ratio 2 : 3. Find the equation of the line.

Solution : Let the required equation of the line be $\dfrac{x}{a} + \dfrac{y}{b} = 1$.

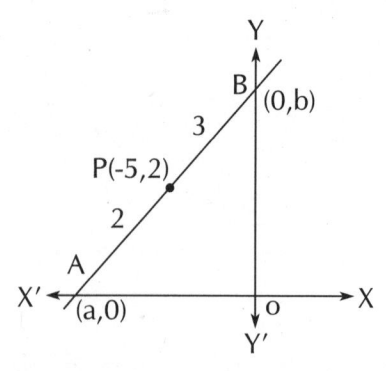

Then, the intercepts made by the line on the x-axis is a and on y-axis is b. P divides the line joining the point A(a, 0) and B(0, b) in the ratio AP : PB :: 2 : 3.

Multiple Choice Questions

1. The side of the tissue box is what shape?

   A. triangle   B. rectangle
   C. square   D. circle

2. The stop sign is what shape?

   A. hexagon   B. octagon
   C. pentagon   D. sphere

3. The map is what shape?

   A. triangle   B. square
   C. circle   D. rectangle

4. The yield sign and the buildings are what shapes?

   A. rectangle and square
   B. triangle and rectangle
   C. cube and triangle
   D. rectangular pyramid and triangle

5. The house is made up of what shapes?

   A. square, triangle, and rectangle
   B. square, circle, and rectangle
   C. square, triangle, and hexagon
   D. square, triangle, and circle

6. The television screen is what shape?

   A. hexagon   B. square
   C. triangle   D. rectangle

7. The center tile is what shape?

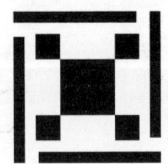

   A. square   B. pentagon
   C. rectangle   D. triangle

Unit - 12 : Geometrical Shapes

8. This tent door is what shape?

   A. circle
   B. square
   C. rectangle
   D. triangle

9. The wheels of the wagon are what shape?

   A. rectangle
   B. triangle
   C. circle
   D. pentagon

10. The black shapes on the soccer ball are what shape?

    A. square
    B. triangle
    C. circle
    D. pentagon

11. I am the shape of a license plate. My shape is also found on refrigerators or windows. What am I?

    A. rectangle
    B. circle
    C. square
    D. triangle

12. I can be found around your yard or even in your bedroom. It's because of me that toys roll and bikes go! I have no sides and no corners. What am I?

    A. rectangle
    B. circle
    C. square
    D. triangle

13. My shape is used for many things, like signs, gift boxes and windows. All my four sides are the same. What am I?

    A. rectangle
    B. circle
    C. square
    D. triangle

14. My shape is found on yield signs and on the frames of a bridge. Although I only have three sides, I can be very strong. What am I?

    A. rectangle
    B. circle
    C. square
    D. triangle

15. Name the shape.

    A. Rectangle
    B. Triangle
    C. Square
    D. Circle

16. Name the shape.

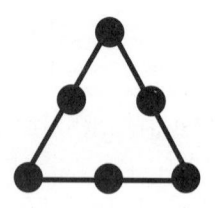

    A. Rectangle
    B. Triangle
    C. Square
    D. Circle

International Mathematics Olympiad – Class 3

17. Name the shape.

    A. Rectangle   B. Triangle
    C. Square   D. Circle

18. Name the shape.

    A. Rectangle   B. Triangle
    C. Square   D. Circle

19. Name the shape.

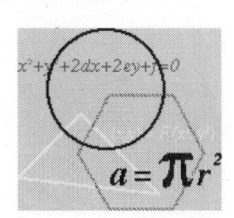

    A. Circle, triangle, hexagon
    B. Square, triangle, hexagon
    C. Rectangle, square, hexagon
    D. Circle, triangle, hexagon

20. What is the shape of this button?

    A. triangle   B. square
    C. octagon   D. circle

21. The equation to the pair of straight lines through the origin which are perpendicular to the lines $2x^2 - 5xy + y^2 = 0$ is.
    A. $2x^2 + 5xy + y^2 = 0$
    B. $x^2 - 5xy + 2y^2 = 0$
    C. $x^2 + 5xy + 2y^2 = 0$
    D. $2x^2 - 5xy + y^2 = 0$

22. If the slope of one of the lines represented by $ax^2 + 2hxy + by^2 = 0$ be the square of the other, then
    A. $a^2b + ab^2 - 6abh + 8h^3$
    B. $a^2b + ab^2 - 3abh + 8h^3$
    C. $a^2b + ab^2 + 6abh + 8h^3$
    D. $a^2b + ab^2 - 6abh - 8h^3$

23. The equation $y^2 - x^2 + 2x - 1 = 0$ represents.
    A. A pair of straight lines
    B. A parabola
    C. A circle
    D. An ellipse

24. The equation $x^2 + ky^2 + 4xy = 0$ represents two coincident lines, if k =.
    A. 0   B. 4
    C. 1   D. 16

25. The angle between the lines given by $x^2 - y^2$ is.
    A. 15^0 B. 75^0
    C. 45^0 D. 90^0

26. The figure has _____ lriangles.

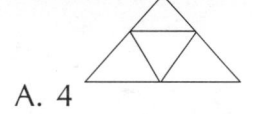

    A. 4   B. 3
    C. 5   D. 2

Unit-12 : Geometrical Shapes

27. The figures has _____ squares.

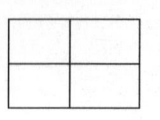

A. 5
B. 4
C. 3
D. 1

28. How many meeting points are there in a square?

A. 4
B. 3
C. 2
D. 1

29. Ruchi built a bird house at summer camp. What shape is the piece of wood that was cut to make the door of the bird house?

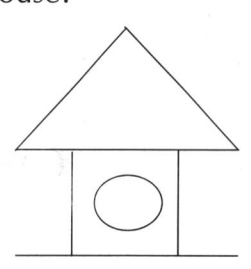

A. Triangle
B. Square
C. Circle
D. Rectangle

30. Matching of columns.

Column A		Column B
1. Square	(i)	△
2. Rectangle	(ii)	○
3. Triangle	(iii)	□
4. Circle	(iv)	▭

A. 1 – i, 2 – ii, 3 – iii, 4 – iv
B. 1 – iii, 2 – iv, 3 – i, 4 – ii
C. 1 – iii, 2 – iv, 3 – ii, 4 – i
D. 1 – ii, 2 – i, 3 – iv, 4 – iii

Answer Key

1. B	2. B	3. C	4. B	5. A	6. D	7. A	8. D
9. C	10. D	11. A	12. B	13. C	14. D	15. A	16. B
17. C	18. D	19. A	20. D	21. C	22. A	23. C	24. B
25. D	26. A	27. A	28. A	29. C	30. B		

Section 2
Logical Reasoning

Unit-1 : Pattern

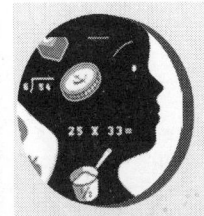

Learning Objectives : In this unit, we will learn about:
- The Concept of Pattern

We use patterns to decide what shapes come next in a design. Look at the design and find the repeated pattern.

The Concept of Pattern

It is a set of shapes, numbers or words that are repeated according to a rule at a regular interval. The basic element of a pattern is a unit which repeats itself.

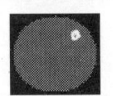

What are the next three shapes in the above pattern?

Ans. The pattern is : square, circle, triangle; square, circle, triangle. So the next three shapes in the given pattern are

We use patterns to decide what numbers come next in a design with a series of numbers. Look at star A. Point number 1 has a value of 4. Go to the next point and look for a number pattern in the star.

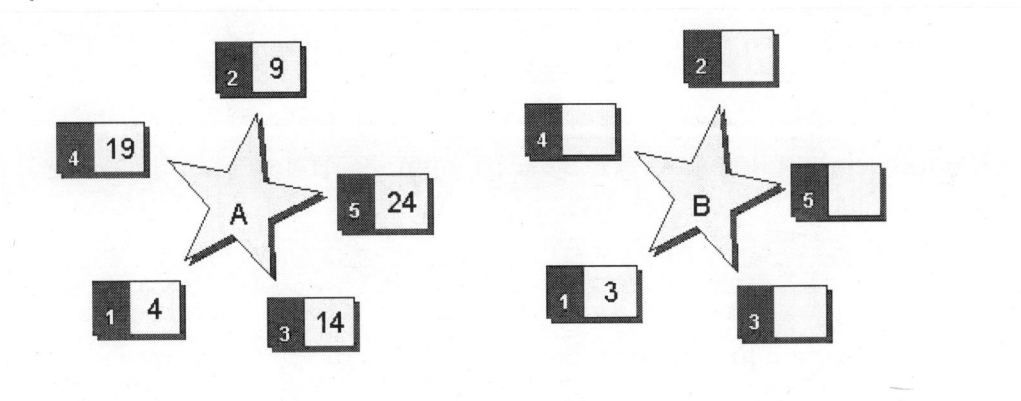

Unit-1 : Pattern

Example : What is the difference between each number? Each number is 5 more than the one before it.

    The first point is 4.
    The second is 9.
    The third is 14.
    The fourth is 19.
    The fifth is 24.

Use the same number pattern to find the next four numbers in star B.

Solution : Start with the first point as 3 and add 5 each time to get the next number. They should be 8, 13, 18, 23.

We use patterns to decide what numbers come next in a series of numbers.

Example : Look for a number pattern.

$$2, 5, 8, 11, \_\_, \_\_, \_\_$$

What is the difference between each number?

Solution : Each number is 3 more than the one before it. Use the number pattern to find the next three numbers.

$$11 + 3 = 14 \quad\quad 14 + 3 = 17 \quad\quad 17 + 3 = 20$$

Hence given series is 2, 5, 8, 11, 14, 17, 20

Example : Look for a number pattern.

$$11, 9, 7, \_\_, \_\_, \_\_,$$

What's the difference between the numbers ?

Solution : Each number is 2 less than the number before. Use the number pattern to find the next three numbers.

$$11 - 2 = 9, \quad 9 - 2 = 7, \quad 7 - 2 = 5, \quad 5 - 2 = 3, \quad 3 - 2 = 1$$

$$11, 9, 7, 5, 3, 1$$

We use number patterns to complete a table. The number pattern is the rule for the table.

IN	2	3	4	5	9	10
OUT	5	6	7			

So, what's the rule? What do you have to do to each IN number to get the OUT number below it?

$$2 + 3 = 5, \quad 3 + 3 = 6, \quad 4 + 3 = 7$$

You add 3 to each IN number to get the OUT number. The rule for this table is Add 3. Use the rule to complete the table. Then write the rule.

IN	2	3	4	5	9	10
OUT	5	6	7	8	12	13

Find the number pattern to complete the table.

IN	11	10	9	5	7	6
OUT	7	6	5			

Here, you subtract 4 from each IN number to get the OUT number.

$$11 - 4 = 7, \quad 10 - 4 = 6, \quad 9 - 4 = 5$$

The rule for this table is Subtract 4.

IN	11	10	9	5	7	6
OUT	7	6	5	1	3	2

Unit – 1 : Pattern

Multiple Choice Questions

1. What are the next two shapes?

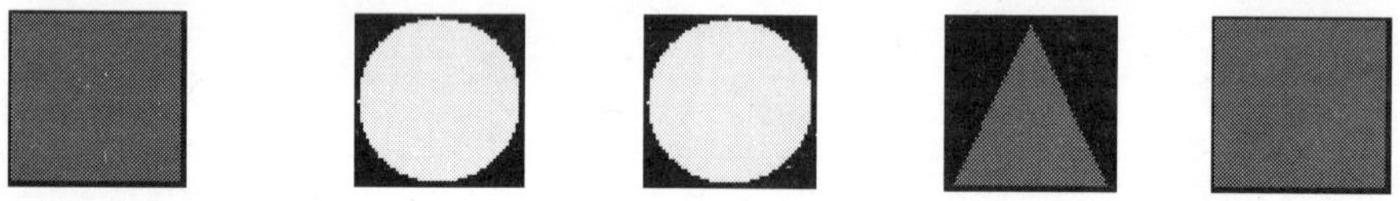

   A. Circle, circle
   C. Circle, triangle
   B. Triangle, circle
   D. Square, circle

2. What are the next two shapes?

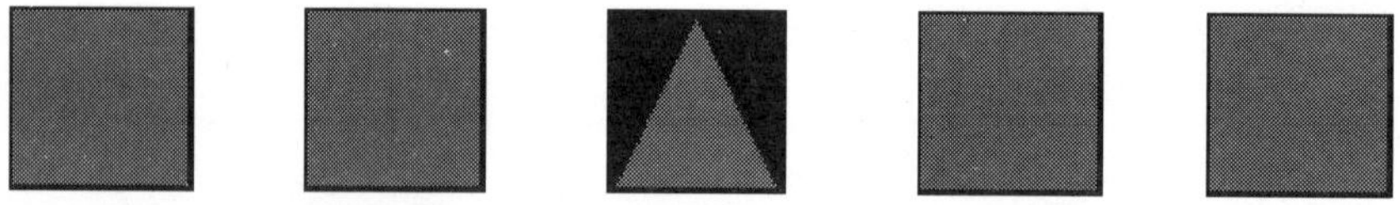

   A. Circle, circle
   C. Circle, triangle
   B. Triangle, square
   D. Square, circle

3. See the number pattern in star A. The first point has a value of 3. Then look a star B. Use the same number pattern to find out the value of the other points.

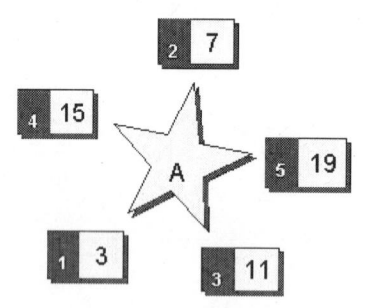

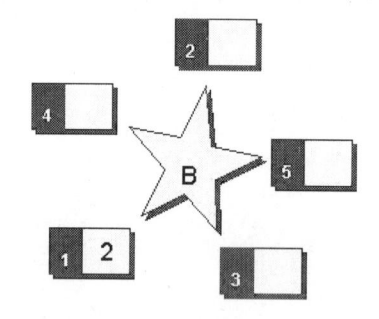

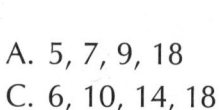

   A. 5, 7, 9, 18
   C. 6, 10, 14, 18
   B. 4, 6, 8, 10
   D. 10, 12, 14, 16

International Mathematics Olympiad – Class 3

4. What number should be on the other points if you follow the same pattern?

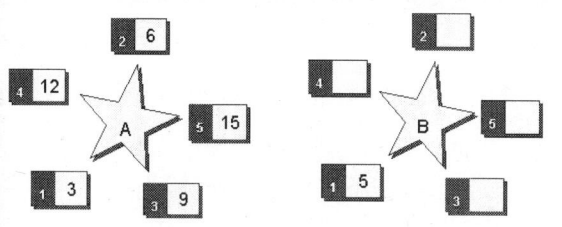

   A. 5, 7, 9, 18
   B. 8, 11, 15, 17
   C. 6, 10, 14, 18
   D. 8, 11, 14, 17

5. Write the next 3 numbers in the following pattern.

   30, 32, 34, ___, ___, ___
   A. 36, 38, 40
   B. 34, 36, 38
   C. 36, 40, 44
   D. None of these

6. What comes next in the following pattern :

   5, 10, 15, ___, ___, ___
   A. 25, 30, 35
   B. 20, 25, 30
   C. 25, 35, 45
   D. 20, 30, 40

7. Find the next 3 numbers in the following pattern :

   27, 24, 21, ___, ___, ___
   A. 15, 12, 10
   B. 20, 19, 18
   C. 18, 15, 12
   D. None of these

8. Write the next 3 numbers in the given pattern.

   24, 20, 16, ___, ___, ___
   A. 10, 8, 6
   B. 4, 6, 8
   C. 6, 10, 14
   D. 12, 8, 4

9. Write the numbers to complete the following table :

IN	2	3	4	5	8	10
OUT	4	5	6			

A. 7, 10, 12
B. 4, 6, 8
C. 6, 10, 14
D. 12, 8, 4

10. Find the numbers to complete the following table :

IN	4	5	6	7	9	10
OUT	8	9	10			

A. 10, 8, 6
B. 11, 13, 14
C. 6, 10, 14
D. 12, 8, 4

11. Write the numbers to complete the following table :

IN	18	17	16	15	10	9
OUT	15	14	13			

A. 10, 8, 6
B. 4, 6, 8
C. 12, 7, 6
D. 12, 8, 4

12. Write the numbers to complete the following table :

IN	28	27	26	25	18	17
OUT	23	22	21			

A. 10, 8, 6
B. 4, 6, 8
C. 6, 10, 14
D. 20, 13, 12

Directions (13-20) : Find the correct missing figures in the following questions:

13.

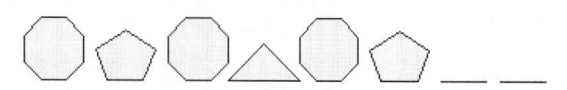

   A. octagon, pentagon,
   B. octagon, triangle.
   C. octagon, octagon,
   D. pentagon, triangle.

14.

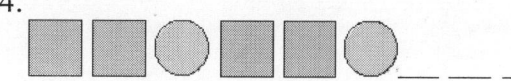

   A. square, circle, square
   B. square, square, circle
   C. circle, circle, square
   D. circle, square, circle

Unit - 1 : Pattern

97

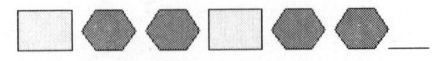

15.
   A. square, hexagon, square
   B. square, square, hexagon
   C. square, hexagon, hexagon
   D. hexagon, square, hexagon

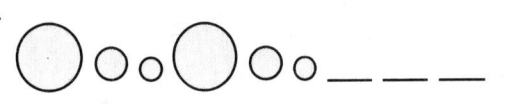

16.
   A. big circle, medium circle, small circle
   B. medium circle, big circle, small circle
   C. big circle, big circle, small circle
   D. small circle, small circle, big circle

17.
   A. circle, circle, pentagon
   B. circle, pentagon, pentagon
   C. pentagon, pentagon, pentagon
   D. circle, pentagon, circle

18.
   A. small rhombus and triangle
   B. big rhombus and triangle
   C. small rhombus and big rhombus
   D. big rhombus and small rhombus

19.
   A. rhombus, triangle, and triangle
   B. rhombus, rhombus, and octagon
   C. rhombus, triangle, and octagon
   D. rhombus, triangle, and rhombus

20.
   A. square, square, and rectangle.
   B. square, rectangle, and rectangle.
   C. rectangle, square, and rectangle.
   D. square, rectangle, and rectangle.

Answer Key

1. A	2. B	3. C	4. D	5. A	6. B	7. C	8. D
9. A	10. B	11. C	12. D	13. B	14. B	15. C	16. A
17. B	18. B	19. C	20. A				

Unit-2 : Series Completion

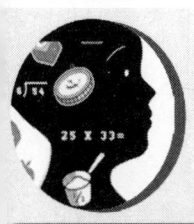

Learning Objectives : In this unit, we shall learn about:
- The Concept of Series Completion
- Tips for Solving Questions on Series

The Concept of Series Completion
In this type of test some numbers and/or alphabetical letters are given. They all form a series and change in a certain order. Series has one or more letters or numbers missing. The candidates are required to observe that specific order in which the number or letters would suit for the blank space if they continue to change in the same order.

Tips for Solving Questions on Series
1. As you solve questions, you will come across many patterns. Solving many questions before the exams will help you pick out patterns faster.
2. Figure can move half distance. For exam the figure can move counter-clockwise (clockwise) 1/2, 1 or 1.5 (and so on) sides in each successive figure.
3. When problem figures repeat use the following tip best applicable when 5 problem figure blocks are given. Compare figure block 1 with 5, if the figure block 5 is identical (or reverse of) figure block 1, the problem figure 2 will be identical (or reverse of) answer figure. This applies to #1 and #4 also in this case #2 will match #5 and #3 will give you the answer figure.
4. When there are many smaller figures in the figure block like, * # @ $ etc. form a matrix and are shifting places and new shapes are replacing old shapes, it may get confusing to deduce the pattern.
5. Do not try to scale the figures, i.e. do not worry about the sizes of lines or shapes unless it is a significant different. They might be drawing errors and there is definitely a much more significant pattern mentioned.
6. The most common pattern is rotation which is asked by itself or in addition with other patterns.
7. Some patterns are established in only the second consecutive image and others are established only in third and fourth consecutive image. Work out your pattern from at least three figures to be sure.
8. Most series questions are simple with one or two types of modifications in the series, i.e. addition, deletion, rotation or modification. Carefully establish the relationship so that you do not miss an important part.

Use the following approach to simplify the question :
   (a) Instead of the shapes name the smaller figures with digits, i.e. in a 3x3 pattern you can name the positions from 1 to 9.
   (b) Begin with elements that are shifting places. Make arrows between positions are shifting places and put a dot for elements that are not changing positions. Solving for more than one figure block can give you significant insight into the pattern
   (c) Now look for new figures replacing old figure. You must note after how many figures the replacement happens.
   (d) Remember that final position can come in more than one step.

Movement of figures
The figures/symbols can move in two directions :
   (i) Clockwise direction
   (ii) Anti-clockwise direction

Rotations of figures
The figures/symbols can rotate at a specific angle either in clockwise or in anticlockwise direction.

9. Basic clockwise and anti-clockwise rotations

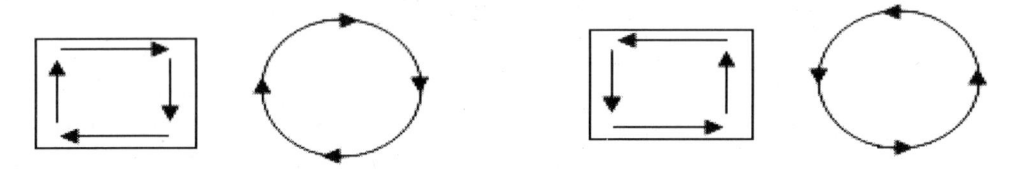

Clockwise rotation   Anticlockwise rotation

10.
   Basic 45° rotations

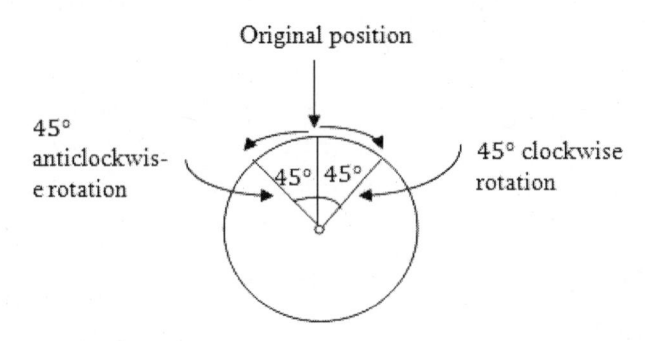

   Original position

   45° anticlockwise rotation   45° clockwise rotation

International Mathematics Olympiad – Class 3

11. Basic 90° rotations

Basic 90° rotations diagram showing Original position, 90° clockwise rotation, and 180° anticlockwise rotation.

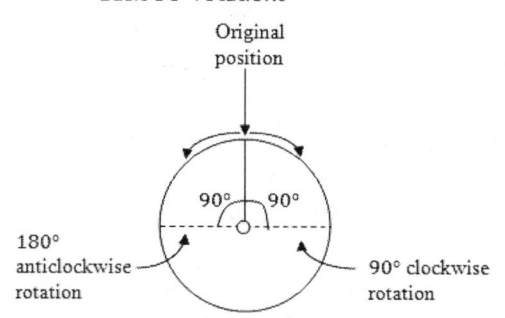

12. Basic 180° rotations

Basic 180° rotations diagram showing Original position, 180° clockwise rotation, and 180° anticlockwise rotation.

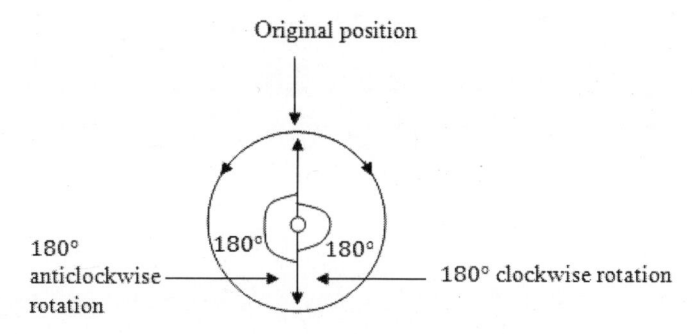

Solved Examples
Example 1 :
Find the next letter in the series;

$$B \ D \ F \ H \ J \ L \ ?$$

   A. N   B. P   C. O   D. M

Answer : A.
Explanation :
The answer is N, because the pattern is to count forward in twos from the first given letter.

$$B + 2 \rightarrow D + 2 \rightarrow F + 2 \rightarrow H + 2 \rightarrow J + 2 \rightarrow L + 2 \rightarrow N$$

Example 2 :
Find the next pair of letters in the series

$$AH \ BI \ CJ \ DK \ ?$$

   A. EL   B. PU   C. OT   D. MS

Answer : A.
Explanation :
The answer is EL, because the pattern is to count forwards in ones for both the fist letter and the second letter :

First letter	A B C D E
Second letter	H I J K L

Answer : (EL).

Example 3 :

Find the missing number in the pattern given below :

$$2 \quad 4 \quad 6 \quad 8 \quad ? \quad 12$$

A. 9
B. 10
C. 11
D. 7

Answer : (B).

Explanation :

$$2 + 2 \rightarrow 4 + 2 \rightarrow 6 + 2 \rightarrow 8 + 2 \rightarrow 10 + 2 \rightarrow 12$$

Hence ? = 10

Example 4 :

Identify the letter which will end the first word and start the second word.

1. CA   ET
   A. U
   B. R
   C. T
   D. N

Answer : (D).

Explanation :

The answer is N because it completes the first word CAN and also begins the second word NET.

Multiple Choice Questions

Direction (1-8) : Find the next letter in the series given below.

1. C D E F G ?
   A. K
   B. J
   C. I
   D. H

2. A D G J M ?
   A. O
   B. P
   C. Q
   D. R

3. D F H J L ?
   A. O
   B. N
   C. M
   D. P

4. F G H I J ?
   A. N
   B. L
   C. K
   D. M

5. C E G I K ?
   A. M
   B. N
   C. O
   D. L

6. Z Y X W V ?
   A. T
   B. U
   C. S
   D. R

7. P M J G D ?
   A. L
   B. B
   C. A
   D. Z

8. W V T Q M ?
   A. F
   B. G
   C. I
   D. H

Direction (9-15) : Find the next pair of letters in the following series :

9. FA GB HC ID JE ?
   A. GL
   B. KF
   C. KG
   D. LH

10. WH TJ QL NN KP JR
    A. IR
    B. JQ
    C. HS
    D. HR

11. HP IR JT KV LX ?
    A. MY
    B. MZ
    C. YL
    D. NZ

12. KU KT LS LR MQ ?
    A. NP
    B. NQ
    C. QM
    D. MP

13. HI IH HJ JH ?
    A. GJ
    B. HK
    C. JG
    D. KH

14. AV BW CX DY ?
    A. DU
    B. EZ
    C. FA
    D. FZ

15. EZ DY CX BW ?
    A. AV
    B. ZU
    C. ZV
    D. AU

Direction (16-20) : Write the number that continues each sequence in the most sensible way.

16. 9 11 14 18 23 ?
    A. 32
    B. 27
    C. 29
    D. 36

17. 13 24 35 46 ?
    A. 57
    B. 68
    C. 69
    D. 67

18. 232 343 454 ?
    A. 545
    B. 565
    C. 656
    D. 575

19. 10, 100, 200, 310, ?
    A. 400
    B. 410
    C. 420
    D. 430

Unit - 2 : Series Completion

20. 11, 10, ?, 100, 1001, 1000, 10001
   A. 101
   B. 110
   C. 111
   D. None of these

Direction (21-25) : Find the missing letters in the following series :

21. EY ? AR
   A. E
   B. P
   C. S
   D. T

22. BA ? AB
   A. C
   B. P
   C. T
   D. M

23. SI ? AP
   A. T
   B. P
   C. O
   D. X

24. TA ? OT
   A. W
   B. E
   C. K
   D. P

25. TW ? NE
   A. S
   B. O
   C. K
   D. N

Answer Key

1. D	2. B	3. B	4. C	5. A	6. B	7. C	8. D
9. B	10. D	11. B	12. D	13. D	14. C	15. B	16. C
17. A	18. B	19. D	20. A	21. A	22. C	23. A	24. D
25. B							

Hints and Solutions

1. The pattern of the series is
   C $\xrightarrow{+1}$ D $\xrightarrow{+1}$ E $\xrightarrow{+1}$ F $\xrightarrow{+1}$ G $\xrightarrow{+1}$ (H)
   ∴ ? = H

2. The pattern of the series is
   A $\xrightarrow{+3}$ D $\xrightarrow{+3}$ G $\xrightarrow{+3}$ J $\xrightarrow{+3}$ M $\xrightarrow{+3}$ (P)
   ∴ ? = P

5. The pattern of the series is
   C $\xrightarrow{+2}$ E $\xrightarrow{+2}$ G $\xrightarrow{+2}$ I $\xrightarrow{+2}$ R $\xrightarrow{+2}$ (L)
   ∴ ? = L

6. The pattern of the series is
   Z $\xrightarrow{-1}$ Y $\xrightarrow{-1}$ X $\xrightarrow{-1}$ W $\xrightarrow{-1}$ V $\xrightarrow{-1}$ (U)
   ∴ ? = U

9. The pattern of the series is

   FA GB HC ID JE KF (with +1 pattern arrows above and below)

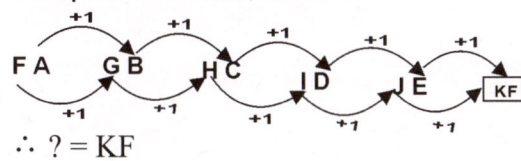

   ∴ ? = KF

14. The pattern of the series is

    AV BW EX DY EZ (with +1 pattern arrows)

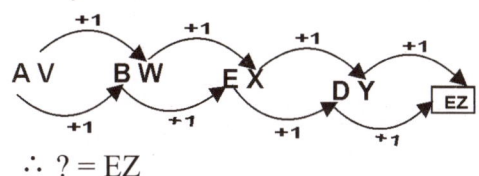

    ∴ ? = EZ

16. The pattern of the given series is
    9 $\xrightarrow{+2}$ 11 $\xrightarrow{+3}$ 14 $\xrightarrow{+4}$ 18 $\xrightarrow{+5}$ 23 $\xrightarrow{+6}$ (29)
    ∴ ? = 29

17. The pattern of the given series is
    13 $\xrightarrow{+11}$ 24 $\xrightarrow{+11}$ 35 $\xrightarrow{+11}$ 46 $\xrightarrow{+11}$ (57)
    ∴ ? = 57

20. The pattern of the given series is
    11 $\xrightarrow{-1}$ 10 $\xrightarrow{-1}$ 101 $\xrightarrow{-1}$ 1001 $\xrightarrow{-1}$
    1001 $\xrightarrow{-1}$ 1000
    ∴ ? = 101

Unit - 2 : Series Completion

Unit-3 : Odd One Out

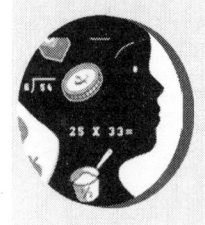

Learning Objectives : In this unit, we will learn about:
- Odd One Out (Classification)
- Types of Classification

Odd One Out (Classification)

Classification is a method of grouping various objects on the basis of their common properties. It helps us to choose the word or pair that different from remaining words of pairs. These questions are designed to test candidate's ability to classify given objects and find one which does not share the common property with the other objects of the group

Types of Classification

The questions on classification are basically of three types as given below:
(a) Words classification
(b) Alphabet classification
(c) Miscellaneous classification

All the possable classifications have been illustrated in the following examples:

Example 1 :

Find the odd one out.

    A. PR   B. CE
    C. WY   D. LM

Answer : (D)
Explanation :
The pattern in option (A), (B) and (C), between the two letters is to count forward in twos whereas in option (D) it is to count forward in ones i.e.,

$$P \xrightarrow{+2} R, C \xrightarrow{+2} E, W \xrightarrow{+2} Y, L \xrightarrow{+1} M$$

Example 2 :

Identify the one which is different from the others.

A. 45 B. 65
C. 85 D. 20

Answer : (D)
Explanation :
All the numbers in options(A) ,(B) and (C) end with 5 except for that in option(D).

Example 3 :
In the question below the letters are linked in some way. Identify the relation and complete the second pair.

BC : DE   KL : MN   PQ : RS   NO : ?

A. QR   B. PQ
C. RS   D. PS

Answer : (B)
Explanation :
BCDE, KLMN, PQRS are consecutive letters in the alphabet. Hence NOPQ is the next pattern.

Example 4 :
Up is down as come is to ?

A. start   B. go
C. after   D. end

Answer : (B)
Explanation :
The answer is go because in the first pair, down is the opposite of up. Similarly in the second pair, go is the opposite of come.

Multiple Choice Questions

1. Find the odd one out.
   A. CD B. KL
   C. EF D. ON

2. Which one is different from the others?
   A. AC B. TU
   C. MO D. XZ

3. Identify the one that does not belong to the group.
   A. POP B. BOB
   C. POT D. TOT

4. Identify the one which is different from the others.
   A. CCD B. FFG
   C. MMN D. VVX

5. Find the odd one out.
   A. YSS B. SYS
   C. SXS D. SSY

6. Which one is different from the others?
   A. 2 B. 4
   C. 7 D. 6

7. Identify the one that does not belong to the group.
   A. 111 B. 222
   C. 383 D. 444

8. Identify the one which is different from the others.
   A. 706 B. 202
   C. 403 D. 302

9. Find the odd one out.
   A. 12 B. 16
   C. 14 D. 51

10. Which one is different from the others?
    A. 456 B. 789
    C. 354 D. 678

11. Identify the one that does not belong to the group.
    A. 255 B. 455
    C. 355 D. 555

12. Identify the one which is different from the others.
    A. Football B. Hockey
    C. Golf D. Basketball

13. Which one is different from the others?
    A. Sunday B. Tuesday
    C. Today D. Thursday

14. Identify the one that does not belong to the group.
    A. Torch B. Bulb
    C. Tube D. Candle

15. Identify the one which is different from the others.
    A. Sword B. Knife
    C. Blade D. Stick

16. Find the odd one out.
    A. Delhi B. Hyderabad
    C. Kolkata D. Srilanka

Identify the relation and complete the last box.

17. A : D   B : E   C : F   X : ?
    A. A B. B
    C. Z D. C

18. A : Z   B : Y   C : X   F : ?
    A. V   B. S
    C. U   D. Q

19. B : Z   E : C   T : R   O : ?
    A. L   B. K
    C. S   D. M

20. PF : FP   ON : NO   LID : ?
    A. PAN   B. RAP
    C. DIL   D. DOT

21. CD : GH   EF : IJ   KL : ?
    A. OP   B. MN
    C. QR   D. RS

22. AA : CC   EE : GG   II : ?
    A. OO   B. JJ
    C. PP   D. KK

23. BDF : HJL   GIK : MOQ   LNP : ?
    A. WYA   B. RTV
    C. TVX   D. SUW

24. BBC : D   CCD : E   AAB : ?
    A. F   B. G
    C. H   D. C

25. MNO : QRS   BCD : FGH   XYZ : ?
    A. ABC   B. DEF
    C. BCD   D. EFG

26. 8 : 11   15 : 18   3 : ?
    A. 7   B. 8
    C. 6   D. 9

27. 7 : 21   8 : 24   3 : ?
    A. 6   B. 9
    C. 12   D. 7

28. 3 : 30   9 : 90   1 : ?
    A. 100   B. 01
    C. 10   D. 001

29. 555 : 555   123 : 321   424 : ?
    A. 444   B. 222
    C. 242   D. 424

30. 101 : 111   111 : 121   505 : ?
    A. 555   B. 525
    C. 515   D. 252

31. 125 : 100   100 : 75   25 : ?
    A. 0   B. 50
    C. 75   D. 100

32. 345 : 567   123 : 345   567 : ?
    A. 123   B. 789
    C. 456   D. 345

33. 10 : 30   100 : 300   1 : ?
    A. 10   B. 6
    C. 3   D. 5

34. 520 : 420   760 : 660   110 : ?
    A. 70   B. 210
    C. 60   D. 10

35. A2 : B3   C4 : D5   E6 : ?
    A. H8   B. F7
    C. F8   D. H7

36. A2 : BB3   C2 : DD3   G2 : ?
    A. II4   B. EE3
    C. HH3   D. F2

In the following questions, the two words in first pair are related. Identify the word that completes the second pair in the most sensible way.

37. DOOR is to HOUSE as LID is to?
    A. Box   B. Top
    C. Screw   D. Open

38. PAGE is to book as WORD is to?
    A. Letter   B. Write
    C. Sentence   D. Read

Unit – 3 : Odd One Out

39. ELBOW is to FINGER as KNEE is to?
   A. Hip
   B. Toes
   C. Hand
   D. Shoulder

40. JASMIN is to JOHN as MANASA is to?
   A. Child
   B. Girl
   C. Youth
   D. Martin

Answer Key

1. D	2. B	3. C	4. D	5. C	6. C	7. C	8. B
9. D	10. C	11. D	12. C	13. C	14. D	15. D	16. D
17. A	18. C	19. D	20. C	21. A	22. C	23. B	24. D
25. C	26. C	27. B	28. C	29. D	30. C	31. A	32. B
33. C	34. D	35. B	36. C	37. A	38. C	39. C	40. D

Hints and Solutions

1. Here C $\xrightarrow{+1}$ D, K $\xrightarrow{+1}$ L, E $\xrightarrow{+1}$ F but O $\xrightarrow{+1}$ P
   ∴ D is correct answer.

3. Here P O P   B O B   P O T   T O T
   Clearly, P O T is different.

4. First two letters are same and then next letter. Clearly VVX is different. VVW (according to pattern)

6. 6 is odd number. 2, 4 and 6 are even numbers.

7. All numbers are same enrapt 383

9. 51 is odd number.

13. Except (C) all are names of days.

16. Silence is a name of country.

17. Here A $\xrightarrow{+2}$ D, B $\xrightarrow{+2}$ E, C $\xrightarrow{+2}$ F and X $\xrightarrow{+2}$ [A]

21. Here CD $\xrightarrow{EF}$ GH, EF $\xrightarrow{CH}$ IJ, KL $\xrightarrow{MN}$ [OP]

22. Here A A $\xrightarrow{+2}$ C C, E E $\xrightarrow{+2}$ G G, then I I $\xrightarrow{+2}$ K K

26. Here 8 $\xrightarrow{+3}$ 11, 15 $\xrightarrow{+3}$ 18, ∴ 3 $\xrightarrow{+3}$ ⑥

27. Here $\frac{21}{7} = 3$, $\frac{24}{8} = 3$ Clearly $\frac{9}{3} = 3$

30. 101 $\xrightarrow{+10}$ 111, 111 $\xrightarrow{+10}$ 121
    505 $\xrightarrow{+10}$ 515

31. 125 $\xrightarrow{-25}$ 100, 100 $\xrightarrow{-25}$ 75, 25 $\xrightarrow{-25}$ 0

38. Book contains pages. Similarly, sentence contains words.

Unit – 3 : Odd One Out

Unit-4 : Coding and Decoding

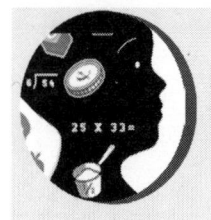

Learning Objectives : In this unit, we will learn about:
- Original Alphabetical Order
- Types of Coding and Decoding

Coding

Coding means the method used to hide the actual meaning of a word or group of words and decoding means the method of making out the actual message that is disguised in coding.

To solve the questions first identify the pattern and then apply it to decode the solution.

Original Alphabetical Order(from left to right)

A	B	C	D	E	F	G	H	I	J	K	L	M
1	2	3	4	5	6	7	8	9	10	11	12	13
N	O	P	Q	R	S	T	U	V	W	X	Y	Z
14	15	16	17	18	19	20	21	22	23	24	25	26

To remember the position of a particular letter in the alphabetical series

The 26 known letters can be easily memorised by (From A to Z) (From Z to A)

E	J	O	T	Y
5	10	15	20	25
V	Q	L	G	B

For example, if we want to find the position of the alphabet 'S', then as we know that 'T' is 20, so 'S' is 20 – 1 = 19. Also, we can find the position of an alphabet from the end by subtracting its value from 27. For example, the position of D from the end is 27 – 4 = 23.

The pattern below is very useful to find many types of question in Alphabet Series when we write the last 13 alphabets in front of the first 13 alphabets of the English:

A	B	C	D	E	F	G	H	I	J	K	L	M
Z	Y	X	W	V	U	T	S	R	Q	P	O	N

Types of Coding and Decoding

The questions on coding and decoding are basically of three types as given below.

Type I. Letter coding

In these questions, code values are assigned to a word in terms of the alphabet and a candidate is required to
  (i) form a code for other word
  (ii) find the word by analysing the given word

1. In a certain code 'SHIMLA' is written as 'RGHLKZ, how will PATNA be coded then?
   A. OZTMZ   B. OZSZM
   C. QBUMB   D. OZTZM

Solution : Each letter is coded as the letter previous to it, i.e. S $\xrightarrow{-1}$ R, H $\xrightarrow{-1}$ G, I $\xrightarrow{-1}$ H, M $\xrightarrow{-1}$ L, L $\xrightarrow{-1}$ K, A $\xrightarrow{-1}$ Z. Similarly PATNA will become OZSMZ. Hence the answer is (B).

2. If CEJQ is coded as XVQJ, then BDIP will be coded as :
   A. WURQ   B. YWRK
   C. WUPI   D. YWPI

Solution : The first 13 letters of the alphabet are coded by the 13 letters of the alphabet in reverse, i.e.

   = A B C D E F G H I J K L M (first 13 letters)
   = Z Y X W V U T S R Q P O N (13 letters in reverse)

It is obvious from the above coding scheme that :
   B = Y, D = W, I = R and K = P or P = K
Therefore, B D I P will be coded as Y W R K.
So, the answer is (B).

Type II. Number coding

In this type of questions, either numerical values alphabetical code values or are assigned to the number.

3. If LODES is coded as 46321, how will you code the word DOES?
   A. 1234   B. 4321
   C. 3621   D. 3261

Solution : Here, you will observe that all the letters of DOES are included in the letters of LODES, for which you have the code D = 3, O = 6, E = 2, S = 1. Therefore DOES = 3621. So, the answer is (C).

4. DAZE is written as 41265 in a certain code. How will BOY be written in the same code?
   A. 41425   B. 5120
   C. 21525   D. 359

Unit–4 : Coding and Decoding   113

Solution : In this question the position of each alphabet is given like D is 4 , Z is 26 etc. So the Code of BOY will be 21525 as B is 2, O is 15 and Y is 25. So, the answer is (C)

Type III. Miscellaneous Types

In this type of questions, three of four messages are given in a code language and candidates are asked to decode such particular word.

5. In a certain code '415' means 'milk is hot'; '18' means 'hot soup'; and '895' means 'soup is tasty'. What number will indicate the word 'tasty'?

   A. 9
   B. 8
   C. 5
   D. 4

Solution : The code for 'hot' is 1. So, the code of 'soup' is 8. Now the code of 'is' is 5. Hence we can say that the code of 'tasty' is 9. So, the answer is A.

6. If 'black' is called 'pink', 'pink' is called 'blue', 'blue' is called 'brown', 'brown' is called 'orange', 'orange' is called 'violet', ' violet' is called 'red' and 'red' is called 'black', what is the colour of blood ?

   A. black
   B. brown
   C. pink
   D. orange

Solution : As the colour of blood is red and red is called black in the given coded language. So the colour of blood is black. Hence the answer is A..

Example :

Each question below is to be coded according to the following letter/ symbol codes.

Number	9	2	5	1	7	5	8	2	2	6
Letter/ Symbol Code										

Number	1	2	3	4	5	6	7	8	9	0
Letter/ Symbol Code	A	P	R	X	*	D	$	N	RS	Q

Now find the letter/ symbol code of given number group.
The first has been done for you as an example.

1.

Number	4	1	0	4	2	9	1	2	1	7
Letter/ Symbol Code	X	A	Q	X	P	RS	A	P	A	$

Try Yourself

2.

Number	1	9	0	5	4	8	7	4	2	6
Letter/ Symbol Code										

3.

Number	9	2	5	1	7	5	8	2	2	6
Letter/ Symbol Code										

Unit-4 : Coding and Decoding

Multiple Choice Questions

Directions (1-11): Capital letters A to Z are given to the table. Under each capital letter a small letter is written which is to be used as a code for the capital letters.

Letter	A	B	C	D	E	F	G	H	I	J	K	L	M	N	O	P	Q	R
Code	n	z	o	y	p	x	Q	w	r	a	s	b	v	c	t	d	u	e

S	T	U	V	W	X	Y	Z
f	m	g	l	h	k	i	J

Based on the table write the codes for the following words.

1. UNIFIED
   A. gcxrrpy   B. gcrxrpy
   C. qcrxrpy   D. grcxpny

2. BMW
   A. nvz   B. lth
   C. znv   D. zvh

3. BRAIN
   A. zenrc   B. eznrc
   C. zenre   D. crrez

4. ALOK
   A. ntsb   B. nbts
   C. nbst   D. tnbs

5. CHAITALI
   A. ownrmnb   B. onwrmnbr
   C. ownrmnbr   D. ownrnmrb

6. SRINIVAS
   A. frecrlnf   B. ferrclnf
   C. fercrlnf   D. efrcrnlf

7. STUDENT
   A. fmgypcm   B. gmfycpm
   C. fgmypcm   D. mcpygmf

8. HYDERABAD
   A. wiypenznt   B. weiypenzns
   C. viyenpzky   D. wiypenzny

9. TENDULKAR
   A. mcpygbsne   B. mpcygbsne
   C. mpcgybsne   D. cpmygbsne

10. REASONING
    A. epnftcrcq   B. penfctrcq
    C. epntfcrcq   D. qcrctfrpe

11. TSUNAMI
    A. mgfncvr   B. mfgcnrv
    C. fmgcnvr   D. mfgcnvr

12. If in a certain language, POPULAR is coded as QPQVMBS, which word would be coded as GBNPVT?
    A. FAMOSU   B. FAMOUS
    C. FASOUM   D. FOSAUM

13. If ROBUST is coded as QNATRS in a certain language, which word would be coded as ZXCMP?
    A. YWBLO   B. YYBNO
    C. AWDLQ   D. AYDNQ

14. If in a certain language, UTENSIL is coded as WVGPUKN, Which word would be coded as DMSFXG?
    A. BKQEVE   B. BKQDWE
    C. BKQDWF   D. BKQDVE

15. If in a certain code, SWITCH is written as TVJSDG, which word would be written as CQFZE ?
    A. BARED
    B. BRAED
    C. BREAD
    D. BRADE

16. In a certain code, REFRIGERATOR is coded as ROTAREGIRFER. Which word would be coded as NOITINUMMA ?
    A. ANMOMIUTNI
    B. AMNTOMUIIN
    C. AMMUNITION
    D. NMMUNITION
    E. None of these

17. If GO = 32, SHE = 49, then SOME will be equal to
    A. 56
    B. 58
    C. 62
    D. 64

18. If AT = 20, BAT = 40, then CAT will be equal to
    A. 30
    B. 50
    C. 60
    D. 70

19. If ZIP = 30 and ZAP = 38, what will be VIP = ?
    A. 174
    B. 43
    C. 34
    D. 113

20. In a certain language, the numbers are coded as follows :

4	3	9	2	1	6	7	8	5	2	0
A	W	P	Q	R	B	E	S	G	J	M

How are the following figure coded in that code ?

421665
A. AQRBBG
B. PQBRSE
C. ASGRBE
D. QRPSSE

21. In a certain language, the numbers are coded as follows :

4	3	9	2	1	6	7	8	5	2	0
A	W	P	Q	R	B	E	S	G	J	M

How are the following figure coded in that code ?

67825
A. BESGJ
B. BSEJG
C. BESJG
D. BSEGJ

22. In a certain language, the numbers are coded as follows :

4	3	9	2	1	6	7	8	5	2	0
A	W	P	Q	R	B	E	S	G	J	M

How are the following figure coded in that code ?

55218
A. GJGRS
B. GGJSR
C. GGRJS
D. GGJRS

23. If bat is racket, racket is football, football is shuttle, shuttle is ludo and ludo is carrom, what is cricket played with ?
    A. Racket
    B. Football
    C. Bat
    D. Shuttle

24. If banana is apple, apple is grapes, grapes is mango, mango is nuts, nuts is guava, which of the following is a yellow fruit ?
    A. Mango
    B. Guava
    C. Apple
    D. Nuts

25. If cushion is called pillow, pillow is called mat, mat is called bedsheet and bedsheet is called cover, which will be spread on the floor ?
    A. Cover
    B. Bedsheet
    C. Mat
    D. Pillow

Unit-4 : Coding and Decoding

Answer Key

1. B	2. D	3. A	4. B	5. C	6. C	7. A	8. D
9. B	10. A	11. D	12. B	13. D	14. D	15. C	16. C
17. A	18. C	19. C	20. A	21. C	22. D	23. A	24. C
25. B							

Hints and Solutions

1. Here U N I F I E D (Using table)
   ↓ ↓ ↓ ↓ ↓ ↓ ↓
   g c r x r p y
   ∴ (B) is correct.

5. C H A I T A L I (Using table)
   ↓ ↓ ↓ ↓ ↓ ↓ ↓ ↓
   o w n r m n b r
   ∴ (C) is correct.

12. Here
    P O P U L A R
    +1↓ +1↓ +1↓ +1↓ +1↓ +1↓ +1↓
    Q P Q V M B S
    Hence
    G B N P V T
    -1↓ -1↓ -1↓ -1↓ -1↓ -1↓
    F A M O U S

14. Here
    U T E N S I L
    +2↓ +2↓ +2↓ +2↓ +2↓ +2↓ +2↓
    W V G P U K N
    Then,
    B K Q D V E
    +2↓ +2↓ +2↓ +2↓ +2↓ +2↓
    D M S F X G

23. Cricket is played with bat. But bat is rocket (according to question)

24. Banana is yellow fruit. Here Banana is Apple.

25. Mat is spread on the floor. Here mat is bed sheet.

Unit - 5 : Alphabet Test and Word Formation

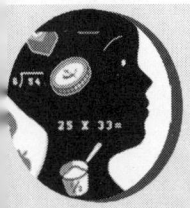

Learning Objectives : In this unit, we will learn about:
- Alphabetical order
- Word Formation

In alphabet test, the questions are based on the understanding of the position of letters in English alphabet. In a dictionary the words are arranged in the alphabetical order. The words beginning with the same letter are again arranged alphabetically with respect to the second letter in the word and so on. In order to solve questions on order arrangement we may have to compare all the letters sequentially.

Alphabetical Order

In this type of questions, certain words are given. The candidate is required to arrange them in the order in which they shall be arranged in a dictionary and then state the word which is placed in the desired place. For such questions, the candidate requires basic knowledge of the 'Dictionary Usage'. In a dictionary, the words are put in alphabetical order with respect to the second alphabet of the words and so on.

Example 1 :
Which letter appears in the word SEVEN, but not in the word NEVER?
   A. M   B. P
   C. S   D. N

Answer : (C)
Explanation :
The answer is S, because the letters E, V and N are in SEVEN and the letters E, V, and N are also in NEVER.
(S is in SEVEN but not in NEVER).

Example 2 :
If the alphabet is written backwards, which letter is in the 20th position?
   A. H   B. G
   C. F   D. T

Answer : (B)

Explanation :

Z X Y W V U T S R Q P O N M L K J I H G F E D C B A

Starting with Z = 1, 20th letter in the above alphabet, the letter in the 20th position is G. Instead of counting from Z (from left), We can also count from A.

20th letter from left is the 7th letter from right i.e. G is the answer.

Word Formation

Some letters from the word in capitals have been used to make other words. In this, questions comes at times in exam.

Example 1 :

Some letters from the word in capitals have been used to make other words. Identify the correct option.

C O N V E N I E N T

A. tonic   B. video
C. nation   D. comic

Answer : (A)
Explanation :

The answer is tonic because the letters of tonic are found in CONVENIENT.

Not 'video' as there is no D, not 'nation' because CONVENIENT has no 'A' and not 'comic' as there is no M in the given word.

Identify the new words that can be formed using the letters of the word in capitals.

Multiple Choice Questions

1. What is the 12th letter of the alphabet?
   A. O B. P
   C. Q D. L

2. Which is the 26th letter of the alphabet?
   A. X B. Z
   C. B D. A

3. If the alphabet is written backwards, which letter is in the 25th position?
   A. Z B. Y
   C. A D. B

4. If the alphabet is written backwards, which letter is in the 15th position?
   A. P B. L
   C. Q D. R

5. Which letter appears in RESIDENT, but not in REINVEST?
   A. D B. V
   C. I D. S

6. Which letter occurs once in FLAG, but twice in APPEARING?
   A. F B. G
   C. P D. A

7. Which letter occurs once in EXERCISE, but twice in SUCCESS?
   A. C B. E
   C. S D. R

8. Which letter occurs twice as often in POTATOES as it does in SILENT?
   A. E B. O
   C. T D. S

9. C O U R T A I N
   A. train B. stain
   C. rent D. track

10. P R E V E N T
    A. seven B. rent
    C. trip D. rest

11. S C R A T C H
    A. chats B. crutch
    C. crate D. care

12. A S S E M B L Y
    A. mess B. slim
    C. bead D. boys

13. H O L I D A Y S
    A. diary B. daily
    C. saint D. sorry

14. L E A R N I N G
    A. angelic B. angry
    C. agent D. angle

15. T O G E T H E R
    A. trot B. rotate
    C. rotten D. then

16. D R A G O N
    A. danger B. near
    C. drag D. gone

17. R E A S O N I N G
    A. right B. new
    C. sitar D. near

18. E X A M I N A T I O N
    A. nest B. nation
    C. maximum D. extra

Unit - 4 : Coding and Decoding

19. Arrange the given words in alphabetical order and choose the one that comes first.
    A. Conceive   B. Diurnal
    C. Conceit   D. Concentrate

20. Arrange the given words in alphabetical order and choose the one that comes first.
    A. Language   B. Laurel
    C. Leisure   D. Lapse

Answer Key

1. D	2. B	3. D	4. B	5. A	6. D	7. A	8. C
9. A	10. B	11. A	12. A	13. B	14. D	15. A	16. C
17. D	18. B	19. C	20. A				

Hints and Solutions

1. A B C D E F G H I J K L M N O P Q R S T U V W X Y Z.
   Clearly 12th letter of the alphabet is L

2. We know 26th letter of the english alphabet is Z.

3. 25th letter from left is B. (or second letter from right)

5. D is not given in REINVEST.

6. A occurs twice in APPEARING.

9. All letters of train is in CURTAIN.

10. All letters of rest is in PREVENT.

19. Conceit comes first in the given word.

20. Language comes first in the given words.

Unit-6 : Problems Based on Figures

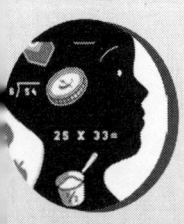

Learning Objectives : In this unit, we will learn about:
- Mirror Image
- Water Image

A figure that can be folded to make equal parts is a symmetrical figure. Line of symmetry is the place where the object can be folded to get equal parts which are mirror images of each other.
Look at the butterfly below. The line of symmetry shows you where you can fold the butterfly
in half to get 2 equal parts.

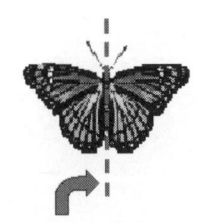

line of symmetry

Note : Symmetrical pattern is the same size, shape, and detail on both sides.
Animals of every shape and size can display bilateral, or mirror images of themselves.

Mirror Image

Reflection of an item into the mirror is called mirror image. It is obtained by inverting an item laterally i.e. towards the sides. It is also known as horizontal plane. Have you ever seen your face in mirror? Basically in mirror right hand becomes left and left hand becomes right. And, your head seems to be same as you thinking right? So that's the trick in mirror image right part of contents appears on left side and left part of contents appears right side but the top upper level and down lower level remains same.

Have a look at the cat to make the concept clear :

Mirror Images of Numbers

1	ɪ
2	ƨ
3	Ɛ
4	₽
5	ट
6	∂
7	ⲅ
8	8
9	ǫ
10	0ɪ

Mirror Images of Alphabets

A	A	H	H	O	O	V	V
B	ꓭ	I	I	P	ꟼ	W	W
C	Ɔ	J	ⳑ	Q	Ọ	X	X
D	ꓷ	K	ꓘ	R	ꓤ	Y	Y
E	Ǝ	L	⅃	S	Ƨ	Z	Ƨ
F	ꟻ	M	M	T	T		
G	ꓱ	N	И	U	U		

Shortcuts and Tricks for Questions on Mirror Image

Alphabetic H, I, M, O, T, U, V, W and X seems to be same but there are much difference between them, only **H, I, O,** and **X**'s mirror images are same

Water Image

The reflection of an item into the water is called water image of that item. It is obtained by inverting an object vertically. Hence Water image is just a reflection where top and bottom part of the image changed where left and right side of image remain same. In Mirror image left side and right side changed vice-versa where top and bottom remain same. See below example to understand in brief.

We can see the dog running on water where his legs reflecting first and head reflecting last both right side and left side remains unchanged.

Water Images of Numbers

1 2 3 4 5 6 7 8 9
I S 3 ᔑ 2 ᓇ ⊥ 8 ᓂ

Number 0 and somehow Number 8 are same in water image reflection. Please note that Number 6 and 9's reflection on water images are same like number 9 and 6 on mirror image.

Water Images of Alphabets

A B C D E F G H I J K L M
∀ B C D E F G H I J K L M

N O P Q R S T U V W X Y Z
N O P Q R S T U V W X Y Z

Seven Alphabets are same in water image : C, D, E, H, I, O, and X. where H, I, O, N, and X are same in mirror image reflection also.

Unit - 6 : Problems Based on Figures

Multiple Choice Questions

1. Choose the alternative which is closely resembles the mirror image of the given combination.

   TERMINATE
   (1) TERMINATE (mirror)
   (2) TERMINATE (mirror)
   (3) TERMINATE (mirror)
   (4) TERMINATE (mirror)

   A. 1   B. 2
   C. 3   D. 4

2. Choose the alternative which is closely resembles the mirror image of the given combination.

   BRISK
   (1) BRISK (mirror)
   (2) BRISK (mirror)
   (3) BRISK (mirror)
   (4) BRISK (mirror)

   A. 1   B. 2
   C. 3   D. 4

3. Choose the alternative which is closely resembles the mirror image of the given combination.

   INFORMATIONS
   (1) INFORMATIONS (mirror)
   (2) INFORMATIONS (mirror)
   (3) INFORMATIONS (mirror)
   (4) INFORMATIONS (mirror)

   A. 1   B. 2
   C. 3   D. 4

4. Choose the alternative which is closely resembles the mirror image of the given combination.

   FIXING
   (1) GNIXIF
   (2) FIXING (mirror)
   (3) FIXING (mirror)
   (4) FIXING (mirror)

   A. 1   B. 2
   C. 3   D. 4

5. Choose the alternative which is closely resembles the mirror image of the given combination.

6. Choose the alternative which is closely resembles the mirror image of the given combination.

   WHITE
   (1) WHITE (mirror)
   (2) WHITE (mirror)
   (3) WHITE (mirror)
   (4) ETIHW

   A. 1   B. 2
   C. 3   D. 4

7. Choose the alternative which is closely resembles the mirror image of the given combination.

   qutubgarh
   (1) qutubgarh (mirror)
   (2) qutubgarh (mirror)
   (3) hragbutuq
   (4) qutubgarh (mirror)

   A. 1   B. 2
   C. 3   D. 4

8. Choose the alternative which is closely resembles the mirror image of the given combination.

   JUDGEMENT
   (1) TNEMEGDUJ
   (2) JUDGEMENT (mirror)
   (3) JUDGEMENT (mirror)
   (4) LUDGEMENT (mirror)

   A. 1   B. 2
   C. 3   D. 4

9. Choose the alternative which is closely resembles the mirror image of the given combination.

   REASONING
   (1) REASONING (mirror)
   (2) REASONING (mirror)
   (3) REASONING (mirror)
   (4) REASONING (mirror)

   A. 1   B. 2
   C. 3   D. 4

10. Choose the alternative which is closely resembles the mirror image of the given combination.

    QUALITY
    (1) QUALITY (mirror)
    (2) YTILAUQ
    (3) YTILAUQ
    (4) YTILAUQ

    A. 1   B. 2   C. 3   D. 4

10. Choose the alternative which is closely resembles the mirror image of the given combination.

    Nu56p7uR
    (1) Ru7p65uN
    (2) Яu56p7uИ (rendered)
    (3) Яu7p65uИ
    (4) Nu56p7uR (rendered)

    A. 1   B. 2
    C. 3   D. 4

11. Choose the alternative which is closely resembles the water-image of the given combination.

    rise
    (1) Lise (rendered)
    (2) esir
    (3) rise (rendered)
    (4) rise (rendered)

    A. 1   B. 2
    C. 3   D. 4

12. Choose the alternative which is closely resembles the water-image of the given combination.

    FAMILY
    (1) FAMILY (rendered)
    (2) FAMILY (rendered)
    (3) FAMILY (rendered)
    (4) FAMILY (rendered)

    A. 1   B. 2
    C. 3   D. 4

13. Choose the alternative which is closely resembles the water-image of the given combination.

    U4P15B7
    (1) U4P15B7 (rendered)
    (2) U4P15B7 (rendered)
    (3) U4P15B7 (rendered)
    (4) U4P15B7 (rendered)

    A. 1   B. 2
    C. 3   D. 4

14. Choose the alternative which is closely resembles the water-image of the given combination.

    96FSH52
    (1) 96FSH52 (rendered)
    (2) 96FSH52 (rendered)
    (3) 96FSH52 (rendered)
    (4) 96FSH52 (rendered)

    A. 1   B. 2
    C. 3   D. 4

15. Choose the alternative which is closely resembles the water-image of the given combination.

    DISC
    (1) CSID
    (2) DISC (rendered)
    (3) DISC (rendered)
    (4) DISC

    A. 1   B. 2
    C. 3   D. 4

16. Choose the alternative which is closely resembles the water-image of the given combination.

    FROG
    (1) FROG (rendered)
    (2) GORF
    (3) FROG (rendered)
    (4) FROG (rendered)

    A. 1   B. 2
    C. 3   D. 4

17. Choose the alternative which is closely resembles the water-image of the given combination.

    wrote
    (1) wrote (rendered)
    (2) wrote (rendered)
    (3) wrote (rendered)
    (4) wrote (rendered)

    A. 1   B. 2
    C. 3   D. 4

18. Choose the alternative which is closely resembles the water-image of the given combination.

    D6Z7F4
    (1) D6Z7F4 (rendered)
    (2) D6Z7F4 (rendered)
    (3) D6Z7F4 (rendered)
    (4) D6Z7F4 (rendered)

    A. 1   B. 2
    C. 3   D. 4

19. Choose the alternative which is closely resembles the water-image of the given combination.

Unit-6 : Problems Based on Figures

monday
(1) yadnom (2) ʎɐbnom
(3) ʎequow (4) wouqɐʎ

A. 1 B. 2
C. 3 D. 4

20. Choose the alternative which is closely resembles the water-image of the given combination.

RECRUIT
(1) ᴚECᴚUIT (2) ᴚECᴚUIT
(3) ᴚECᴚUIT (4) ᴛIUᴚCEᴚ

A. 1 B. 2
C. 3 D. 4

21. Find out the alternative figure which contains figure (X) as its part.

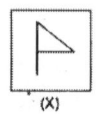

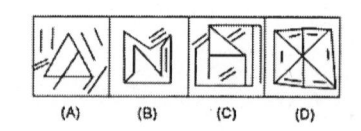

A. A B. B
C. C D. D

22. Find out the alternative figure which contains figure (X) as its part.

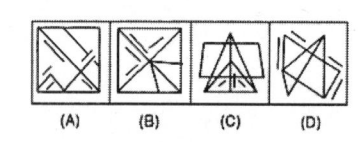

A. A B. B
C. C D. D

23. Find out the alternative figure which contains figure (X) as its part.

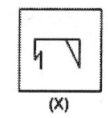

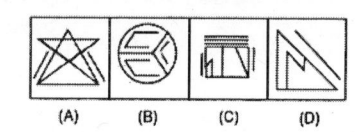

A. A B. B
C. C D. D

24. Find out the alternative figure which contains figure (X) as its part.

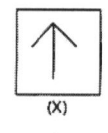

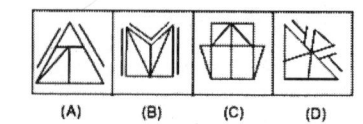

A. A B. B
C. C D. D

25. Find out the alternative figure which contains figure (X) as its part.

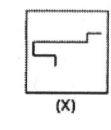

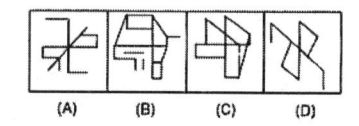

A. A B. B
C. C D. D

Answer Key

1. C	2. D	3. C	4. D	5. C	6. D	7. C	8. B
9. C	10. C	11. A	12. D	13. C	14. C	15. C	16. A
17. C	18. C	19. D	20. B	21. C	22. A	23. C	24. C
25. B							

SECTION 3
ACHIEVERS SECTION

High Order Thinking Skills

1. Number of corners in 4 squares and 5 triangles is _____.
   A. 23
   B. 31
   C. 20
   D. 18

2. Which of these has the smallest value?
   A. 1/2 of 160
   B. Half of 180
   C. 12 × 13
   D. 2 times of (5 × 5)

3. A pizza was cut into 8 equal pieces. Kusum ate 3 pieces. What fraction of the pizza is left with her?
   A. 3/8
   B. 4/8
   C. 5/8
   D. 3/4

4. How many two-digit numbers between 10 to 40 have the digits at ten's place smaller than that of one's place?
   A. 19
   B. 20
   C. 21
   D. 22

5. Which of the following has same value as 2618?
   A. 200 + 618
   B. 2000 + 600 + 18
   C. 2000 + 68
   D. 2008 + 17

6. In a school there were 2349 pupils. 251 new pupils were admitted into the school and 169 pupils left the school during the year. How many pupils were there in the school at the end of that year?
   A. 3486
   B. 2600
   C. 2431
   H. 2180

7. In Shweta's school, the lunch time is between 12:15 pm and 1:30 pm. What is the duration of the lunch time?
   A. 1 hr 05 minutes
   B. 1 hr 15 minutes
   C. 1 hr 20 minutes
   D. 1 hr

8. Nandani and Suman bought 345 stickers. Sid bought 65 more stickers than Armaan. How many stickers did Armaan buy?
   A. 140
   B. 150
   C. 145
   D. 130

9. Choose the correct option:
   A. 371 > 231
   B. 591 < 326
   C. 140 > 200
   D. 529 = 226

10. Golu is 25 years old. His brother Ankit is 4 years elder to him. How old is Ankit?
    A. 21 years
    B. 29 years
    C. 22 years
    D. 24 years

11. Which number makes the equation true ?
    66 – ? = 80 – 32
    A. 68
    B. 18
    C. 58
    D. 38

12. Rahul and Rohit wrote a total of 678 words. If Rahul wrote 253 words, how many words did Rohit write?

A. 425 words B. 525 words
C. 931 words D. 831 words

13. Kusum reads 26 page of a book in one day. How many pages can she read in 4 days?
    A. 100 B. 105
    C. 104 D. 108

14. Saurav multiplied 3 with a number and found an answer. His friend Ashish made 9 groups of a number and found that his answer is same as Saurav answer so he shared it with her sister Tina. Tina told Ashish that he has just interchanged the numbers multiplied by Saurav. Can you find the answer that both Saurav and Ashish found?
    A. 30 B. 29
    C. 28 D. 27

15. 50 bubble gums are shared equally among seven children. How many bubble gums are left over?
    A. 1 B. 2
    C. 3 D. 4

16. Ashima clicked 24 pictures. She distributed them equally in 8 friends. How many picture does each friend has?
    A. 8 B. 4
    C. 3 D. 24

17. Which two fractions are equivalent?
    A. 1/2 and 1/3 B. 6/2 and 12/4
    C. 1/4 and 1/6 D. 2/3 and 1/3

18. In May, Richa earned ₹ 10 everyday for helping her mother in doing house hold work. She spent ₹ 95. How much she is left with?
    A. ₹ 215 B. ₹ 180
    C. ₹ 200 D. ₹ 310

19. Suman went for shopping at 12:00 pm. She came back at 4:00 pm. How much time did Suman spent shopping?
    A. 3 hours B. 2 hours
    C. 4 hours D. 1 hour

20. If in a certain language, UTENSIL is coded as WVGPUKN. Which word would be coded as DMSFXG?
    A. BKQDVE B. BKQDWE
    C. BKQDWF D. BKQDVF

Answer Key

1. B	2. D	3. C	4. C	5. B	6. C	7. B	8. A
9. A	10. B	11. B	12. A	13. C	14. D	15. A	16. C
17. B	18. A	19. C	20. A				

Section 4
Model Papers

Model Test Paper – 1

Section I Logical Reasoning

1. If ⌂+△ stands for 15 and △△△△ stands for 24.

   What do ⌂⌂⌂⌂△ stands for?
   A. 24
   B. 40
   C. 18
   D. 42

2. What fractions of the faces are smiling in the given figure?

   A. 10/24
   B. 7/24
   C. 9/24
   D. 11/24

3. Complete the number sequence given below.

   5987, 5753, _____, 5285, 5051
   A. 5529
   B. 5521
   C. 5519
   D. 5419

4. How many more parts should be shaded to make the figure 4/5 shaded?

   A. 5
   B. 4
   C. 3
   D. 2

5. What is the difference between the number of shaded triangles and the number of unshaded triangles in pattern 100?

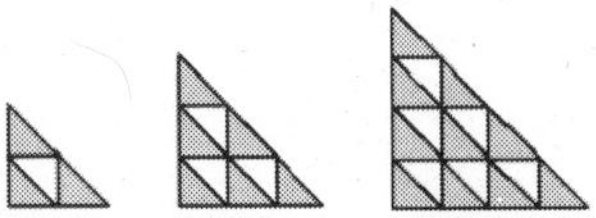

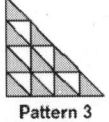

   Pattern 1 Pattern 2 Pattern 3

   A. 99
   B. 100
   C. 101
   D. 1000

6. Which of the following shows the correct order from the greatest to the smallest?
   A. 117, 118, 119
   B. 886, 888, 890
   C. 224, 324, 424
   D. 976, 956, 936

7. What is the product of 9 and 3?
   A. 7 tens 2 ones
   B. 2 tens 7 ones
   C. 2 tens 4 ones
   D. 27 tens

8. Which one of the shapes given below has the largest portion shaded?

   A. 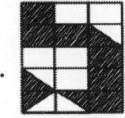
   B. 
   C. 
   D.

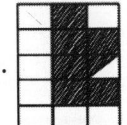

9. Find the sum of 567 and 3456. Which digit is in the hundreds place of the sum.?
   A. 0
   B. 1
   C. 2
   D. 3

Model Test Paper – 1

135

10. Match the figure given in Column I to the lengths given in Column II

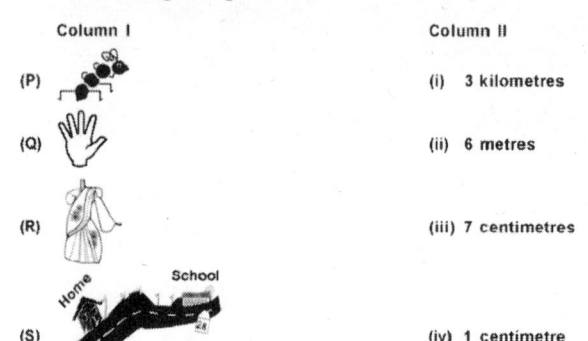

Column I	Column II
(P)	(i) 3 kilometres
(Q)	(ii) 6 metres
(R)	(iii) 7 centimetres
(S)	(iv) 1 centimetre

A. P - (iv), Q - (iii), R - (ii), S - (i)
B. P - (iii), Q - (iv), R - (i), S - (ii)
C. P - (iv), Q - (iii), R - (i), S - (ii)
D. P - (iii), Q - (iv), R - (ii), S - (i)

11. How many triangles are present in the given figure?

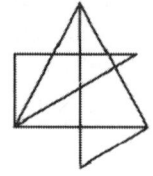

A. 10   B. 11
C. 15   D. 18

12. Bincy was born on 2nd May in the year 2005. How old will she be on 2nd May in the year 2052?
A. 40   B. 47
C. 48   D. 49

Direction (13-16): The graph given below shows how the pupils travel from home to school. Study the graph carefully and answer the questions.

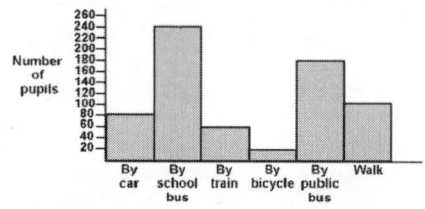

13. What is the total number of pupils who travel by the school bus and by the train?
A. 60   B. 180
C. 240   D. 300

14. How many more pupils travel by public bus than by Car?
A. 80   B. 100
C. 180   D. 260

15. The number of pupils who travel by train is 3 times that of the number of pupils who travel by _____.
A. Car   B. School Bus
C. Public Bus   D. Bicycle

16. If 36 girls travel to school by train, how many boys travel by train?
A. 24   B. 36
C. 60   D. 84

17. 9 × 7 does not have the same value as _____.
A. 7 + 7 + 7 + 7 + 7 + 7 + 7 + 7 + 7
B. 9 + 9 + 9 + 9 + 9 + 9 + 9
C. 20 + 20 + 20 + 13
D. 70 – 7

18. A frog jumps 3 steps at a time.
A squirrel jumps 4 steps at a time.
A rabbit jumps 6 steps at a time.

How many jumps of the frog are equal to two jumps of the rabbit?
A. 2   B. 4
C. 9   D. 12

19. A man saw 5 cockroaches. How many legs did he see?

   A. 30   B. 20
   C. 40   D. 25

20. Observe the pattern given below:

   14A, 16C, 19F, 23J, ...

   What comes next in the pattern?
   A. 25L   B. 28O
   C. 27N   D. 24K

21. What fraction of the insects are 🐜 ?

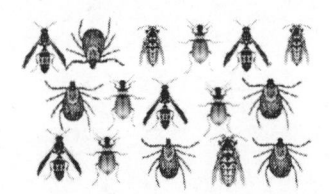

   A. 4/16   B. 3/16
   C. 5/16   D. 6/16

22. The Map (not drawn to scale) shows 4 different ways of going from Town X to Town Y. The shortest way of going Town X to Town Y is through Town _____.

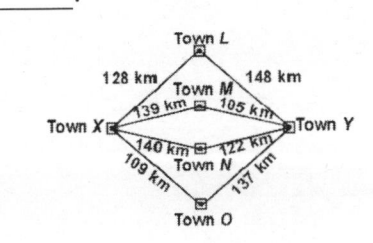

   A. L   B. M
   C. N   D. O

23. [6 Thousands 9 Hundreds and 1 Ten] – [3 Thousands 2 Hundreds and 5 Tens] = [3 Thousands 6 Hundreds and X Tens]. Then value of X is _____.
   A. 5   B. 60
   C. 6   D. 40

24. What fraction of the given figure is not shaded?

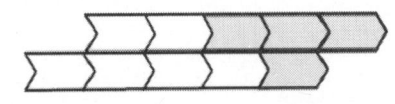

   A. 6/10   B. 4/10
   C. 7/10   D. 1/10

25. Arun is eating a cake. He ate 4/5 of the cake. What fraction of cake is left with him?
   A. 4/5   B. 3/5
   C. 1/5   D. 2/5

Directions (26-28) : The table given below shows the monthly salaries of 4 men.

Name	Rajat	Rohit	Danny	Peter
Salary	Rs.2000	Rs.1800	Rs.1600	Rs.1200

26. What is the difference between Rohit's and Peter's salary?
   A. ₹ 600   B. ₹ 800
   C. ₹ 200   D. ₹ 1600

27. If Rajat spends ₹ 1750 from his salary every month and saves the rest, how much will he save in a year?
   A. ₹ 250   B. ₹ 400
   C. ₹ 2000 D. ₹ 3000

28. If Peter's salary is increased by Rs 400, then Peter's salary will be equal to the salary of which person?
   A. Rajat   B. Rohit
   C. Danny   D. None of these

Model Test Paper – 1

29. How many squares form 2/3 of the rectangles?

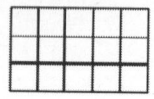

   A. 2 squares   B. 3 squares
   C. 5 squares   D. 10 squares

30. Which one of the following has the greatest value?
   A. 6 Thousands 3 Hundreds 0 Tens 9 Ones
   B. 6 Thousands 3 Hundreds 9 Tens 0 Ones
   C. 6 Thousands 0 Hundreds 0 Tens 9 Ones
   D. 6 Thousands 9 Hundreds 9 Tens 3 Ones

31. Fill in the boxes with the digits 0, 1, 2, 3, 4, 5, 6, 7, 8 or 9 to make

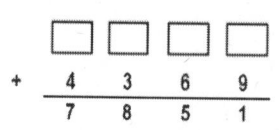

   ```
     □ □ □ □
   +   4 3 6 9
   ─────────────
     7 8 5 1
   ```

   A. 8, 4, 2, 1   B. 3, 4, 8, 2
   C. 9, 2, 1, 0   D. 4, 3, 1, 1

32. Taking 5 Hundreds from 3819 gives _____.
   A. 3319   B. 3814
   C. 3824   D. 4319

33. What is the mass of the teddy bear shown in figure ?

   A. 400 g   B. 450 g
   C. 300 g   D. 600 g

34. Which of the following is the longest?
   A. 4 m 8 cm   B. 480 cm
   C. 5 m 14 cm   D. 540 cm

35. Peter is 167 cm tall. His sister is 29 cm shorter than Peter. What is the total height of Peter and his sister?
   A. 1 m 38 cm   B. 1 m 96 cm
   C. 3 m 5 cm   D. 3 m 63 cm

Model Test Paper – 2

SECTION I – LOGICAL REASONING

1. Which is the ninth object?

   A. (flamingo)   B. (tortoise)
   C. (car)   D. (sunflower)

2. In the given picture grid which word describes the position of ◇ ?

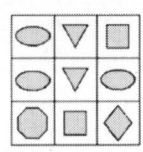

   A. Top centre   B. Top left
   C. Bottom right   D. Centre left

3. If you look at this object from the top, what will you see?

   A.   B.
   C.   D.

4. Look at this pattern
   △ ? ? ? ☆ ◇ △ ☆ ◇ △ ☆ ◇ . Which is the missing part?

   A. ☆ ◇ △   B. △ △ △
   C. ☆ △ △   D. ☆ ☆ ☆

5. What is the least whole number you can make using all the following number?

       3 5 1
   A. 135   B. 315
   C. 531   D. 351

6. The Tiger scored fewer points than the Dolphins but more points than Eagles. Which team has scored the most points?
   A. The Dolphins
   B. The Eagles
   C. The Tigers
   D. Both Tigers and Dolphins

7. Rohit has the given amount of money shown here. If the prices shown include Tax, which one of the following shirts can be buying with this money?

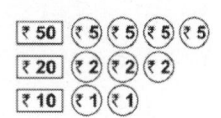

   ₹50 ₹5 ₹5 ₹5 ₹5
   ₹20 ₹2 ₹2 ₹2
   ₹10 ₹1 ₹1

   A. ₹ 100   B. ₹ 150
   C. ₹ 180   D. ₹ 145

8. Look at the given Venn diagram. How many are hearts but not green?

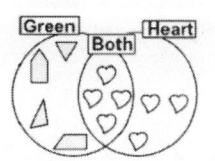

   A. 3   B. 4
   C. 5   D. 6

Model Test Paper – 2   139

9. Rahul needs new toothpaste and some toothpaste. He can choose from the toothbrush colors and toothpaste flavors shown in the picture.

   How many different combinations of 1 toothbrush color and 1 toothpaste flavor are possible

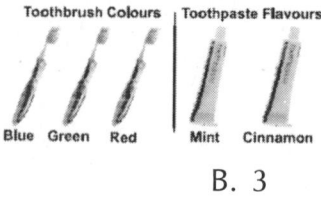

   Toothbrush Colours: Blue Green Red
   Toothpaste Flavours: Mint Cinnamon

   A. 2
   B. 3
   C. 5
   D. 6

10. Third grade students made maps of Main Street. They used symbol for each office building, park and house.

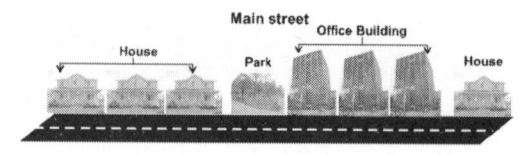

    Main street — House, Park, Office Building, House

    Which equation could be used to find out how many more office buildings are there than parks?

    A. 3 + 1 =
    B. 4 + 3 =
    C. 3 + 1 =
    D. 1 + 4 =

11. Which of the following figures is similar to the given figure?

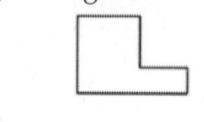

    A.   B.   C.   D.

12. Which number sentence matches the given picture?

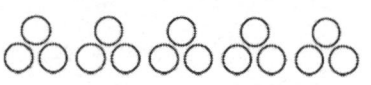

    A. 3 + 5
    B. 15 + 3
    C. 5 X 3
    D. 15 X 3

13. Look at Gaurav's timeline. What happens after Gaurav cleans the cabin and before he plays sand volleyball?

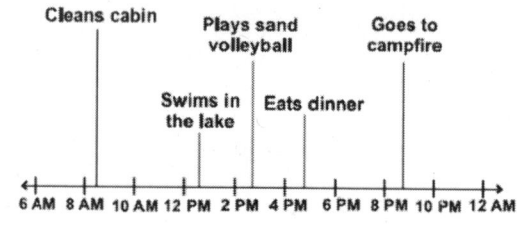

    Cleans cabin | Swims in the lake | Plays sand volleyball | Eats dinner | Goes to campfire
    6 AM 8 AM 10 AM 12 PM 2 PM 4 PM 6 PM 8 PM 10 PM 12 AM

    A. Gaurav goes to the campfire.
    B. Gaurav eats Dinner.
    C. Gaurav swims in the lake.
    D. None of these.

14. Parul put 70 plastic cups in the first stack, 80 plastic cups in the second stack, and 90 plastic cups in the third stack. If this pattern continues, how many plastic cups will Parul put in the fourth stack?

    A. 100
    B. 108
    C. 106
    D. 107

15. How has this figure been transformed?

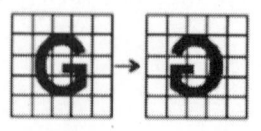

    It has been _____
    A. Reflected
    B. Rotated
    C. Translated
    D. None of these

16. Which instrument you would use to find out how long will the train to arrive at the station?

    A. Clock
    B. Thermometer
    C. Tape Measure
    D. Ruler

17. Yesterday was Wednesday. What day is tomorrow?
    A. Thursday
    B. Friday
    C. Saturday
    D. Sunday.

18. Look at the given pattern.

    ◯◯♥◯◯♥◯◯♥

    How would you show this pattern using letters?
    A. AAB
    B. AB
    C. ABC
    D. ABB

19. Divya spent 1 week at a summer camp. What is the total number of days in 1 week?
    A. 7
    B. 2
    C. 5
    D. 8

20. Look at these numbers: 6 66 71 76 Which two numbers above have a sum of 137?
    A. 6 and 66
    B. 71 and 66
    C. 6 and 76
    D. 66 and 76

21. If a month ends on a Tuesday, on what day does the next month begin?
    A. Thursday
    B. Monday
    C. Wednesday
    D. Tuesday

22. Which of the given shapes represents a rectangle?

    A. (square)
    B. (trapezoid)
    C. (circle)
    D. (triangle)

23. The distance around the middle of the Earth is 2757 kilometers. What is the place value of the digit 2 in the number 2757?
    A. 200
    B. 20
    C. 2
    D. 2000

24. Pulkit is having a birthday party. His mother told him that he could divide 30 stickers among the 4 friends he has invited. If pulkit gives each friend the same number of stickers, which picture shows how many stickers each friend will get?

    A.
    B.
    C.
    D.

25. The length of a shirt sleeve is best measured in_____
    A. Inches
    B. Millimeters
    C. Liters
    D. Grams

26. 1 2 3 4 5 6 7 8 9 10 11 12 13 14 15 16 17 18 19 20 21 22 23 24 25 26 27 28 29 30 31 32 33 34 35 36 37 38 39 40

    Shally crosses out the numbers she says as she counts by 5(5, 10, ----) Next she will cross out all the even numbers on the chart above. Which one of the following number will she Not cross out?
    A. 20
    B. 23
    C. 35
    D. 38

ıdel Test Paper - 2

141

27. What is the missing number that makes the number sentence true?

   ? + 19 + 7 = 33

   A. 6
   B. 7
   C. 58
   D. 59

28. What is another way to represent 6,204?

   A. 6+2+0+4
   B. 60+20+10+4
   C. 600+200+100+4
   D. 6000+200+4

29. Which letter can be folded in half, so that its side coincides?

   A. W
   B. N
   C. L
   D. S

30. Which is the closest distance from point M to point N on the number line?

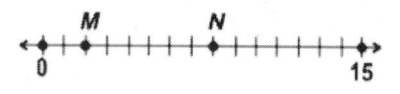

   A. 5 units
   B. 8 units
   C. 7 units
   D. 6 units

31. The clock shows the time 12:45. What time will it show after 45 min?

   A. 1:30
   B. 2:15
   C. 1:45
   D. 12:00

32. I am greater than 250 but less than 280. When you add my first and third digits you will get 9. Which number am I?

   A. 257
   B. 254
   C. 279
   D. 269

33. Rohan and Arjun played a Basketball game. They scored a total of 10 baskets. If Rohan scored 7 Baskets, then how many Baskets did Arjun score?

   A. 3
   B. 5
   C. 7
   D. 9

34. Romesh has 19 eggs. He has 2 empty egg cartons that can hold 12 eggs in each carton. How many more egg does Romesh need to fill the 2 egg cartons?

   A. 7
   B. 24
   C. 33
   D. 5

35. A snail can crawl 30 inches in 1 minute, if the snail crawls at this speed in one direction for 6 minutes, how far in inches, will it travel?

   A. 240 inches
   B. 180 inches
   C. 36 inches
   D. 5 inches